PROTECTED LANDSCAPES

The United Kingdom Experience

Prepared by

Duncan and Judy Poore

for the

**Countryside Commission
Countryside Commission for Scotland
Department of the Environment for Northern Ireland**

and the

International Union for Conservation of Nature and Natural Resources

Published for the

International Symposium on Protected Landscapes
Lake District, United Kingdom
5-10 October 1987

Published in 1987 as a contribution to
the European Year of the Environment

and the Council of Europe's
Campaign for the Countryside

by

Countryside Commission, Countryside Commission for Scotland, Department of the Environment for Northern Ireland and the International Union for Conservation of Nature and Natural Resources

Additional copies available from:

Countryside Commission
Publications Despatch Department
19/23 Albert Road
Manchester M19 2EQ, UK

Price: £6.50

This publication is a companion volume to *Protected Landscapes: Experience around the World* to be published by the International Union for Conservation of Nature and Natural Resources, with the support of British Petroleum.

Cover photographs: Snowdonia National Park, Wales; Lake District National Park, England; Causeway Area of Outstanding Natural Beauty, Northern Ireland; Cuillin Hills (Isle of Skye) National Scenic Area, Scotland.

Credits: The publishers thank the following for the use of their photographs: The National Trust in Northern Ireland (Giant's Causeway, cover); Duncan Poore (Skye, cover); the Trustees of the National Museums and Galleries on Merseyside, Walker Art Gallery (Wilson painting of Snowdon) and Terry Symonds (Cotswolds).

Other photographs reproduced with kind permission of the Countryside Commission, Countryside Commission for Scotland and the Department of the Environment for Northern Ireland.

ISBN 2-88032-925-6
CCP 233

Printed by Ebenezer Baylis & Son Ltd, Worcester, UK

CONTENTS

PREFACE

The British Isles are small, long settled and crowded. This long occupation means that there are no true wilderness areas and almost all our landscapes bear the indelible impression of man's continuous habitation, farming and industrial activities. But the landscapes created often have great beauty and charm and the British have a strong emotional relationship with their countryside. One consequence has been a consistent national desire, initially led by non-governmental organisations - but for the last 40 years also accepted by government - to prevent undesirable and destructive development in the countryside and to conserve the best of it for the nation to enjoy. The way this has been achieved, through the designation of protected landscapes, is the subject of this book.

The term "protected landscape" is taken from the International Union for Conservation of Nature and Natural Resources (IUCN). IUCN advises that countries should establish a range of protected area types, amongst which is Protected Landscapes (Category V), whose purpose it is "to maintain nationally significant, natural landscapes which are characteristic of the harmonious interaction of man and land, while providing opportunities for public enjoyment through recreation and tourism within the normal life-style and economic activity of these areas". The areas described in this Directory, and especially the national parks of England and Wales, illustrate the IUCN concept well. They also equate to the Council of Europe's similar Classification C of protected areas.

What distinguishes the UK approach to conserving important landscapes is the acceptance that not only will established land uses, principally agriculture, continue but that the maintenance of many of those landscapes depends on sustaining traditional farming practice. Also, there is an implicit recognition of the contribution which the way of life of the local people makes to the enjoyment of the area by tourists. The inspirational quality of such cultural landscapes is best illustrated by the place of the Lake District - currently a candidate for World Heritage status - in the history of art, literature, conservation and tourism, but each protected landscape displays a remarkable example of "the harmonious interaction of man and land".

The objectives of this directory are two-fold:

- to illustrate the variety of scenery and natural resources which are protected in the United Kingdom, and

- to show how protection is achieved in practice.

We aim to provide both domestic and international audiences with an account of the distinctive way in which we protect the finest landscapes of the United Kingdom. Whilst this is not an account of nature conservation - for which there are separate arrangements - the systems of landscape protection and nature conservation in the UK are mutually supportive. Thus, many national nature reserves and sites of special scientific interest contribute to the conservation of protected landscapes, and the reverse is also true.

We have published the Directory to coincide with the International Symposium on Protected Landscapes being held in the English Lake District in October 1987. Together, the Symposium and Directory will, we believe, make a significant contribution to an appreciation of the United Kingdom's experience and what it may offer to other countries. This Directory is also a companion to *Protected Landscapes: Experience around the World* published by IUCN as a further contribution to the Symposium.

This Directory is a collaborative venture between the Countryside Commission (England and Wales), the Countryside Commission for Scotland, the Department of the Environment for Northern Ireland and IUCN. The other sponsors wish to thank IUCN for undertaking the compilation.

In addition the compilers wish to acknowledge the assistance given by national park officers, the Nature Conservancy Council, the National Trust and the National Trust for Scotland, and the staff of both Countryside Commissions and the Department of the Environment for Northern Ireland. The information contained in this Directory is accurate as of 1 June 1987; we regret that it has been impossible to include any amendments after this date.

An introduction to the British landscape

There can be few countries in the world which have so rich a variety of landscape in such a small compass as the United Kingdom. The tempestuous breakers and soaring seabirds of St Kilda on the Atlantic seaboard and the ice-laden winds sweeping over the high plateau of the Cairngorms or the ridges of Snowdon provide all the wildness and challenge that anyone may wish. An early summer morning on a New Forest lawn with the mists rising over the water, grazing deer and the sun dappled shade under ancient oaks is the rural idyll of many folk. The harmony between village architecture in softly blending traditional materials and the pattern of fields bordered by stone walls backed by the outlines of an Iron Age hillfort give a sense of peace and the continuity of rural life. Britain has all of these: the rocks, the bones of the landscape, span all epochs from the pre-Cambrian to the most recent; there are glaciated and un-glaciated land forms (though no glaciers); our position on the Atlantic fringe of Europe and the great range of latitude (from 48 to 62 degrees) lead to a wide variety of climates and moods - from the wet and blustery November day in the west, to the vast arching skies of continental East Anglia and the cool, clear light of the long days of the northern summer in the Shetlands. And, over all, the traces of the past are evident wherever they have not been covered by later buildings or effaced by the plough.

> Many things are encompassed in our understanding of the word landscape: the geological structure of the land, its soils, animals and its vegetation; the patterns of human activity - fields, forests, settlements and local industries - both past and present. It is a matter not only of beauty, of aesthetic appreciation of nature and architecture, but of the whole ecology of an area and the history of its occupation and use by people.

"Snowdon seen from across Llyn Nantlle", Richard Wilson, 1776. The appreciation of our native scenery was emerging in the latter half of the eighteenth century. Wilson's painting of wild Snowdonia (despite the pastoral figures) played an important part in opening people's eyes and minds to the natural beauty of our landscape.

For the whole of the United Kingdom has been moulded to some extent by human occupation. The traces are very slight, it is true, high in the mountains or on the remoter parts of the coast; at certain seasons there it is possible to get the illusion of complete wilderness. There is very little in Britain that can honestly be said to conform to the international ideal of the national park. Yet there are landscapes of the very highest quality, as is evidenced by the millions that come to visit them every year, landscapes of such value to the nation that their character must be safeguarded. These are all lived in and used and most are privately owned; even the high moors and the remote islands are used for economic purposes - indeed much of the character of most of them depends upon continuing habitation and use.

Here lies the dilemma; how to preserve the character of these landscapes - and to make them available to be enjoyed - in a world of changing economic pressures and social conditions.

This is not a matter for Britain alone; a high proportion of the natural beauty and diversity in the world occurs in areas which are used by Man. Indeed the protection and management of such areas is the main objective of IUCN in establishing its Category V of Protected Landscape. The management objectives of this category are defined as:

"To maintain nationally significant natural landscapes which are characteristic of the harmonious interaction of man and land while providing opportunities for public enjoyment through recreation and tourism within the normal life-style and economic activity of these areas. These areas also provide for ecological diversity, scientific, cultural and educational purposes."

We are confident that the ways in the which the United Kingdom has tackled these problems will have interest and value elsewhere in the world.

How the British landscape is protected

The concept

The concept is very simple. In a country where most of the land is privately owned and is used by people for their livelihood, ownership by the State is not a possible answer; protection has to be achieved in more subtle ways.

The means adopted, therefore, are on the one hand the control of development and, on the other, incentives to favour beneficial kinds of land management. At the same time various categories of land have been established by statute which are subject to a graded system of controls and attract different incentives - the most important, the national parks, are subject to the most powerful measures. In addition, special arrangements have been made in the national parks for a management authority to design policies and coordinate action.

This system, though complicated, has three great advantages:

- it can grow within the framework of existing policies and legislation;

- it places the responsibility for protection (within national guidelines) firmly with the people who live in and use the countryside; and

- it is flexible; changes in the degree of control or of incentive can be readily introduced without fundamental changes in the law; and it has been possible to adopt different approaches to suit conditions in England, Scotland, Wales and Northern Ireland.

Legislation

The main measures which are the foundation of present policies for landscape protection were designed during the Second World War as part of national plans for post-war reconstruction and they became law in the late 1940s.

Undoubtedly the most significant for their effects on the British countryside were the Acts of Parliament dealing with planning (the Town and Country Planning Act 1947 for England and Wales and the parallel Acts for Scotland and Northern Ireland). With their subsequent amending legislation, these form the basis for all regional and local planning and for the control of development. Planning authorities were established which have been given the duty of preparing "structure plans" and "local plans"; these lay down the main lines for future development. Also, most physical developments can only proceed after planning permission for them is granted by the planning authority; there is provision for a public inquiry if there are objections; and controversial cases can be referred to the Secretary of State.

At the same time a number of reports were commissioned by the Government on aspects of the use and conservation of the countryside, notably by John Dower, a great advocate of national parks, and by committees chaired by Sir Arthur Hobhouse, and by Sir Douglas Ramsay for Scotland. There were separate reports devoted to nature conservation.

The main outcome of this work was the National Parks and Access to the Countryside Act 1949 which provided the foundation for the British system of protected areas, both for landscape and for nature conservation - a system which has been added to and refined in later years but never fundamentally changed.

In the field of landscape protection the 1949 Act provided for two categories of protection: **National Parks** and **Areas of Outstanding Natural Beauty** (AONB). These provisions of the Act only became effective in England and Wales and the National Parks Commission set up to implement them only operated in England and Wales. Scotland and Northern Ireland followed different courses.

Principal legislation affecting protected areas

England and Wales

National Trust Acts 1907,1919, 1937, 1939, 1953 & 1971
Town and Country Planning Act 1947
National Parks and Access to the Countryside Act 1949
Countryside Act 1968
Town and Country Planning Act 1971
Local Government Act 1972
Nature Conservancy Council Act 1973
Ancient Monuments and Archaeological Areas Act 1979
Local Government Planning and Land Act 1980
Wildlife and Countryside Act 1981 (and Amendment Act 1985)
Mineral Workings Act 1985
Agriculture Act 1986

Scotland

National Trust for Scotland Order Confirmation Acts 1935, 1938, 1947, 1952,
    1961 & 1973
Town and Country Planning Act (Scotland) 1947
National Parks and Access to the Countryside Act 1949
Countryside (Scotland) Act 1967
Town and Country Planning (Scotland) Act 1972
Local Government (Scotland) Act 1973

Northern Ireland

Amenity Lands Act (Northern Ireland) 1965: superseded by
Nature Conservation and Amenity Lands (Northern Ireland) Order 1985
Planning (Northern Ireland) Order 1972

In the field of nature conservation, which is closely allied to landscape protection and complements it in many ways, three categories were established: **National Nature Reserves (NNR)**, **Local Nature Reserves (LNR)** and **Sites of Special Scientific Interest (SSSI)**. The Nature Conservancy was established to operate the national policy for nature conservation not only in England and Wales, but also in Scotland. Measures for Northern Ireland followed later.

Since then these categories have played a fundamental national role in effective landscape conservation - all of them in England and Wales, the NNR and SSSI in Scotland.

The ten areas which were selected under the 1949 Act as prospective national parks were all in

Categories of protected landscape

The various kinds of protected landscape that have been mentioned above will be described in detail in the remainder of this booklet. Here we give an outline of their main characteristics.

National Park (England and Wales) - designated by the Countryside Commission.

"A national park may be defined, in application to Great Britain, as an extensive area of beautiful and relatively wild country in which, for the nation's benefit and by appropriate national decision and action:

- the characteristic landscape beauty is strictly preserved;
- access and facilities for public open-air enjoyment are amply provided;
- wildlife and buildings and places of architectural and historic interest are suitably protected; while
- established farming use is effectively maintained."

John Dower, 1945

National Scenic Areas NSA (Scotland) - identified by the Countryside Commission for Scotland and designated by the Secretary of State for Scotland.

"Areas . . . . of national scenic significance . . which . . . we consider to be of unsurpassed attractiveness which must be conserved as part of our national heritage."

Countryside Commission for Scotland, 1978

Areas of Outstanding Natural Beauty AONB (England and Wales) - designated by the Countryside Commission.

"Parts of the countryside of England and Wales which, while they lack extensive areas of open country suitable for recreation and national park status, are nonetheless of such fine landscape quality that there is a national as well as a local interest in keeping them so."

Countryside Commission, 1983

Areas of Outstanding Natural Beauty AONB (Northern Ireland) - designated by the Department of the Environment (Northern Ireland).

"An extensive area of countryside within which the outstanding natural and cultural landscapes demand policies to safeguard their quality and to promote their enjoyment by the public."

upland Britain with the exception of the Pembrokeshire Coast. Various proposals for areas in the lowlands were not accepted (some of these have now become AONBs). But there were two of very special importance, the New Forest and the Norfolk and Suffolk Broads, which are considered to be equivalent in quality to national parks. These, because of their special status and problems, have been the subject of their own legislation and special arrangements.

A number of areas had been proposed by the Ramsay Committee as national parks for Scotland. When it was decided not to apply the national park provisions of the 1949 Act to Scotland these were named "National Park Direction Areas" in which special planning conditions were to apply. These areas have now been embraced within the category of **National**

Heritage Coasts (England and Wales) - defined by the Countryside Commission and specified in local authority structure plans.

"A non-statutory designation covering 'selected areas of undeveloped coastline'."

Countryside Commission, 1987

Environmentally Sensitive Areas ESA (United Kingdom) - designated by the Minister of Agriculture.

"Areas of national environmental significance whose conservation depends on the adoption, maintenance or extension of a particular form of farming practice; in which there have occurred, or there is a likelihood of, changes in farming practices which pose a major threat to the environment; which represent a discrete and coherent unit of environmental interest; and which would permit the economical administration of appropriate conservation aids."

Ministry of Agriculture Fisheries and Food, 1987

The following categories of land are protected for nature conservation rather than landscape; they often contribute, however, to landscape protection:-

Sites of Special Scientific Interest SSSI (England, Scotland and Wales) - notified by the Nature Conservancy Council (NCC).

"Any area of land [which, in the opinion of the Nature Conservancy Council] is of special interest by reason of its flora, fauna, or geological or physiographical features."

Area of Special Scientific Interest ASSI - notified by the Department of Environment, Northern Ireland.

Comparable to the SSSI.

National Nature Reserve NNR (England, Scotland, Wales) - declared by the Nature Conservancy Council.

Land of national importance being managed as a nature reserve by the NCC, under an agreement with the NCC or by an approved body.

National Nature Reserve NNR (Northern Ireland)

Land of national importance managed as a nature reserve by the Department of the Environment for Northern Ireland, under agreement with the Department or by an approved body.

Scenic Area (NSA) which was adopted in 1978 as the principal category for landscape protection in Scotland.

In Northern Ireland three categories have been adopted: AONB, NNR and **Area of Special Scientific Interest** (ASSI) corresponding closely to the SSSI of England, Scotland and Wales.

The early policies were framed on the assumption that conservation of the landscape was fully compatible with existing methods of farming, although there was some concern about the extension of forestry plantations. Most of the checks and balances were associated with physical developments such as new buildings, roads, quarries and power stations which required planning permission under the planning Acts. But it became apparent in the 1960s and 1970s that the changing intensity and structure of agriculture and the great expansion of forestry planting were at least as important in changing the landscape, affecting access and in leading to a decline in habitat for wildlife. The Porchester Report on Exmoor highlighted the problem in relation to the ploughing of moorland to provide better grazing for stock.

This led to the introduction of the Wildlife and Countryside bill which gave an unprecedented amount of parliamentary exposure to the question. The resulting Wildlife and Countryside Act 1981 introduced a number of very important measures affecting protected landscapes and SSSI. In the case of landscape, it empowered the relevant authority to enter into management agreements with owners or occupiers of land "so as to conserve or enhance the natural beauty or amenity of the land or promote its enjoyment by the public"; it gave power to the Secretary of State for the Environment, together with the Minister of Agriculture, to prohibit the conversion of moor and heath into agricultural land if it had not been so in the preceding 20 years; and there were other similar measures.

In the case of SSSIs the constraints were even stronger. The NCC was required to notify the owners and occupiers of any SSSI and to provide them with a list of operations likely to damage the special interest. Any person intending to carry out any of these operations must give the NCC notice of their intention. The NCC would then enter into negotiations with them with the aim of concluding a compensatory management agreement. Similar provisions apply in Northern Ireland where the role of the Nature Conservancy Council is taken by the Department of the Environment for Northern Ireland.

To this concern over the changes in landscape brought about by agriculture is now added the very serious question of farm surpluses in Europe and migration from the remoter parts of the countryside. This has led to proposals to use funds for agricultural support to help farmers to adopt practices that are kind to landscape and to wildlife. The result is the designation of eight Environmentally Sensitive Areas, and the Government has announced its intention of designating six more.

Responsibilities

There are differences in the organisation of landscape protection in the various parts of the United Kingdom. In England the main responsibility lies with the Secretary of State for the Environment; but in Scotland, Wales and Northern Ireland it is exercised by the respective Secretaries of State for those countries. The responsible authority in England and Wales is the Countryside Commission for England and Wales, which became the successor to the National Parks Commission with wider responsibilities under the Countryside Act 1968. In Scotland the Countryside Commission for Scotland is responsible, established in 1967 under the Countryside (Scotland) Act. In Northern Ireland action was delayed until 1965 when responsibilities for both nature conservation and landscape protection were given to the Department of the Environment by the Amenity Lands (Northern Ireland) Act, now superseded by the Nature Conservation and Amenity Lands (Northern Ireland) Order, 1985. Thus the principal organisations concerned at country level are the two Countryside Commissions and the Conservation Service of the Department of the Environment for Northern Ireland.

A crucial part is played in the operation of the whole system by local government - the county councils, regional councils, local and district councils.

The two Countryside Commissions and the Department of the Environment for Northern Ireland develop policies and standards; they identify the various categories of protected area; and they have the power to disburse money to further their policies. The two Countryside Commissions too, being independent statutory bodies, can bring influence to bear on the Government to change policies that they feel are harmful to their cause. The Countryside Commissions work largely with the local authorities in whose areas the national parks or other protected areas occur. Only in two national parks, the Peak District and the Lake District, is there a special planning authority for the park; for all other national parks decisions are made by a statutory national park committee of the county council (or one of the county councils where more than one county is affected).

In England, Scotland and Wales an important supplement to the work of the Countryside Commissions is provided by the Nature Conservancy Council (NCC), the successor in 1973 to the Nature Conservancy. The Sites of Special Scientific Interest (SSSIs) selected by the NCC are proving to have a very special importance in preserving natural features which are often also of importance for landscape and there is, not surprisingly, a considerable overlap between them; for example in England and Wales the national parks contain over 1800 sq km which have been notified as SSSI (over 13 per cent of the area of the parks) and the AONB over 690 sq km (4 per cent).

In contrast to the two Countryside Commissions, the Nature Conservancy Council is a land-holding agency; although it has very close relations with the local authorities, it owns and manages its own nature reserves and is directly responsible for negotiating management agreements to secure the value and integrity of the SSSI.

Archaeological monuments, traces of prehistoric occupation and buildings of historical or architectural merit are also important features of the landscape. These are the responsibility in England of the Historic Buildings and Monuments Commission for England (English Heritage); of the Historic Buildings and Monuments Directorate of the Scottish Development Department in Scotland, and of the Conservation Service of the Department of the Environment in Northern Ireland. There are various categories: Scheduled Ancient Monuments, Listed Buildings and Conservation Areas (groups of buildings of special merit in towns and villages) which are afforded special protection.

There are many other organisations which contribute to the protection of landscape in different ways. Among the most important are the National Trust (operating in England, Wales and Northern Ireland) and the National Trust for Scotland. They were pioneers in the field; the National Trust was founded in 1895 and among its first purchases were areas in what is now the Lake District National Park. The Trusts own substantial areas of beautiful country, often in national parks or other protected landscapes, and many buildings of great merit. Their purposes conform completely with the objectives of landscape protection. Those of the National Trust

Areas of protected landscapes (May, 1987)		
Designation	Number	Area/length
National Parks	10	13,745 sq km
Equivalent areas	2	662 sq km
National Scenic Areas (Scotland)	40	10,018 sq km
AONBs (England & Wales)	37	17,084 sq km
AONBs (Northern Ireland)	9	2,803 sq km
Heritage Coasts*	40	1,370 km
Environmentally Sensitive Areas* (England and Wales only)	6	1,800 sq km

* These can be found within the previous categories.

for Scotland, for example, contain the following phrases: ". . for the purposes of promoting the permanent preservation for the benefit of the nation of lands and buildings in Scotland of historic or national interest . . . and as regards lands for the preservation (so far as practicable) of their natural aspect and features and animal and plant life . . .". Land held by the National Trusts can be declared "inalienable" and cannot be sold by the Trusts or acquired from them without special parliamentary procedure.

Land is also acquired and managed for conservation purposes by local authorities and by many voluntary organisations: for woodland preservation by the Woodland Trust; for nature conservation by the many local Naturalists Trusts associated together in a broad federation with the Royal Society for Nature Conservation and, in Scotland, by the Scottish Wildlife Trust; for birds by the Royal Society for the Protection of Birds.

Strong advocacy for landscape protection is provided by the Council for the Protection of Rural England (CPRE) and its sister bodies in Wales (CPRW), Scotland (the Association for the Protection of Rural Scotland) and Northern Ireland (the Ulster Society for the Preservation of the Countryside). The cause of the national parks is especially promoted by the Council for National Parks, a national umbrella organisation representing more than 30 voluntary bodies.

Conclusion

In this field nothing stands still. One can expect continuing changes in the social and economic forces which bear upon the people who live in the British countryside, which in turn will alter the ways in which they affect the landscape. Landscape protection requires constant vigilance and the continual revision of the measures required to protect. The combination of measures adopted in Britain seem to have a stregth and flexibility that may prove able to respond adequately to these challenges. Only time will tell.

NATIONAL PARKS AND EQUIVALENT AREAS

(England and Wales)

The most beautiful, spectacular and dramatic expanses of country in England and Wales have been given the status of national park by Parliament in recognition of their importance. There are ten national parks ranging in size from 583 to 2,279 square kilometres; Brecon Beacons, Dartmoor, Exmoor, the Lake District, Northumberland, the North York Moors, the Peak, the Pembrokeshire Coast, Snowdonia and the Yorkshire Dales. But there are, in addition, two areas with special characteristics and histories, which are not national parks but are recognised as being of comparable quality: the New Forest and the Broads. Descriptions of all these follow.

The national parks have been established under the National Parks and Access to the Countryside Act, 1949.

- Their first aim is to provide protection for the countryside while also taking care of the distinctive ways of life found within them.

- Their second aim is to provide opportunities for relaxation and outdoor recreation.

The National Parks Commission was set up by the 1949 Act to designate areas as national parks and to advise on their running. In 1968 it became the Countryside Commission (for England and Wales), keeping those responsibilities along with new ones for the countryside as a whole.

The parks are "national" in the vital sense that they are of special value to the whole nation because of their beauty and the opportunities they provide for leisure; in a crowded and long-inhabited country such as Britain there cannot be found pristine areas of country undisturbed by Man, such as are required by the IUCN definition of national parks. The rich patterns of our landscape were created by farmers and landowners over many generations and today the land still remains largely in their hands. Nearly a quarter of a million people live in national parks which are living, working landscapes with many local communities. They correspond exactly to the types of landscape envisaged by the IUCN Category V.

Each park is administered by a park authority. In two instances, the Peak and the Lake District, a special authority has been set up to administer the park; in the remaining national parks the authority is a committee of the county council or a joint committee of more than one council, if the park crosses the boundary between counties. The national interest is reflected in several ways: one third of the members are appointed by Ministers; three quarters of the running costs are met by central government; and the Countryside Commission provides a national oversight of the status of national parks. The Broads are administered by a special authority set up by Act of Parliament; and the New Forest by the Forestry Commission under a specific mandate from the Minister of Agriculture.

NATIONAL PARKS

NAME	Area sq km	Date designated	Residents (thousand)	Visitor days (million)
Brecon Beacons	1350	1957	32.0	7.0
Dartmoor	945	1951	30.0	7.8
Exmoor	686	1954	10.0	2.5
Lake District	2280	1951	40.0	12.0
Northumberland	1031	1956	2.5	1.0
North York Moors	438	1952	25.0	11.0
Peak	1404	1951	40.0	20.0
Pembrokeshire Coast	583	1952	22.0	12.5
Snowdonia	2170	1951	25.0	7.5
Yorkshire Dales	1761	1954	16.8	8.5

NATIONAL PARKS - BUDGETS

NAME OF PARK	BUDGET			
	Total (£ million)	Central %	Local %	Self-gen %
Brecon Beacons	0.7	75	25	0
Dartmoor	1.39	59	33	8
Exmoor	0.98	75	25	0
Lake District	2.62	49	16	35
Northumberland	0.57	72	11	17
North York Moors	0.99	75	25	0
Peak	3.71	58	19	23
Pembrokeshire Coast	1.49	67	17	16
Snowdonia	1.75	75	13	?
Yorkshire Dales	1.47	60	20	20

Budgets are for 1986/7 except for Exmoor which is for 1987/88

NATIONAL PARKS - PERMANENT STAFF

Brecon Beacons	36
Dartmoor	49
Exmoor	39
Lake District	104
Northumberland	45
North York Moors	51
Peak	142
Pembrokeshire Coast	63
Snowdonia	88
Yorkshire Dales	62

The national parks are facing constant threats caused by the social and economic conditions of the nation as a whole, such as:

- changes in agriculture;
- increased afforestation;
- demands for mineral extraction;
- building of new roads and upgrading of old ones;
- the need of land for military training;
- water and power schemes;
- pressure for development;
- loss of local employment;
- increasing visitors;
- inadequate funds.

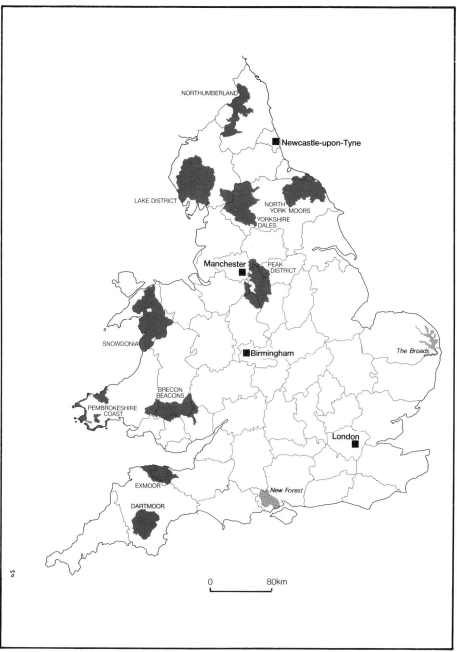

National Parks and equivalent areas in England and Wales

At present the most topical are the changes in the whole structure of rural land use brought about by agricultural over-production within the EEC which hold out new hope for protected landscapes in the United Kingdom. Issues such as this are taken up at the national level by the Countryside Commissions, among others, and their representations may lead to significant changes in government policies.

More specifically, the aims of the national parks are met in two main ways:

1. The national park authorities are the authorities responsible for **planning** matters and can therefore strongly influence any decisions made about physical developments in the park. They can, and do, oppose any developments within a park which they judge will harm its quality as landscape.

2. They can also do much to influence the **management** of the land and attitudes to landscape by many measures: negotiating agreements on land management and access for the public; planting and managing broadleaved woodlands; assisting in the upkeep of paths, fences and stone walls (the Upland Management Service); buying land to protect its traditional character; encouraging small-scale industrial, commercial and tourist development which meets local needs and fits into the scene; advising on grants for farmers who wish to retain traditional features; setting up information centres, car parks, picnic areas and, in some areas, simple overnight accomodation; employing rangers to help and advise visitors; publishing a wide range of books and leaflets; arranging talks and guided walks; running training and field study courses; encouraging volunteers to undertake conservation work in the parks; and operating a youth and schools liaison service.

Other organisations with similar aims do much to help. Large parts of the parks are scheduled as SSSI and are therefore subject to all the restraints on use and open to opportunities for conservation management that are the responsibility of the Nature Conservancy Council under the Wildlife and Countryside Act, 1981; some parts of parks are managed as national or local nature reserves. The National Trust also has considerable land holdings in the parks.

The national parks, the New Forest and the Broads are working examples of how landscapes in IUCN Category V can be protected. They demonstrate how planning controls, flexible incentives for conservation management and goodwill may be used to retain the qualities of these landscapes in a changing world.

Brecon Beacons National Park

Designated 1957   1,350 sq km

Description

The Brecon Beacons National Park lies in South Wales (parts of counties of Dyfed, Gwent, Mid-Glamorgan and Powys), north of Swansea, Cardiff, Newport and Merthyr Tydfil. It contains the most impressive mountains in southern Britain and those nearest to London, consisting of a north-facing escarpment broken only by the fertile Usk valley. The extensive uplands, much over 1000 feet (305 m), are composed of ancient sedimentary rocks. Some of the mountains have markedly flat tops where they are capped with resistant conglomerate. In the glaciated corries great sweeps of scree fall from the cliffs. In the centre are the Beacons, a fine series of peaks, with a magnificent four mile ridge crowned by Corn Du and Pen y Fan (886 m) the highest summit in the park. The wild Black Mountain and the ancient royal hunting ground of Fforest Fawr lie to the west. To the north east the broad valley of the Usk separates the Beacons from the Black Mountains which stretch to and across the English border. To the south, Carboniferous Limestone and Millstone Grit underlie a contrasting landscape of deep-cut gorges and caves; sink holes and waterfalls give national importance to the park.

Much of the upland is common land, covered with moorland vegetation and subject to extensive grazing. Arctic-alpine plants, many of them at the southern limits of their range in Britain, form communities on ungrazed crags. The woods and scrub on the limestone cliffs and steep valley sides contain many interesting plants and have a number of rarities including one endemic sub-species of whitebeam (Ley's whitebeam). Twenty per cent of the park is considered to be of national importance for nature conservation.

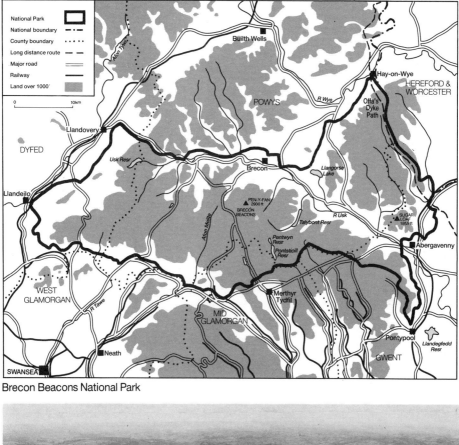

0   10km

Builth Wells

Hay-on-Wye

HEREFORD &
WORCESTER

POWYS

R Wye

Offa's
Dyke
Path

Afon Tywi

DYFED

Llandovery

Usk Resr

Brecon

Llangorse
Lake

SUGAR
LOAF
1955 ft

Llandeilo

PEN-Y-FAN
2906 ft
BRECON
BEACONS

R Usk

Abergavenny

Afon Mellte

Talybont Resr

Pentwyn
Resr

Pontsticill
Resr

WEST
GLAMORGAN

R Tawe

MID
GLAMORGAN

Merthyr
Tydfil

Pontypool

Llandegfedd
Resr

GWENT

Neath

SWANSEA

Brecon Beacons National Park

The central ridge to Corn Du in the Brecon Beacons, the highest mountains in southern Britain. The upland plateau of sedimentary rocks with steep slopes and the glacial lake below contrast with the lowland landscape of enclosed fields.

This is an area of stock farming. Livestock bred on the hill farms are sent to the lowlands for fattening. The hedged and walled fields, interspersed with small patches of deciduous woodland, make an attractive contrast to the open moors above. There are nearly 1000 small woods of native broadleaved trees, many of them unmanaged, which stand in sharp contrast to the large areas of commercial forestry scattered throughout the park. These plantations (covering 8.6 per cent of the park area), together with the 19 reservoirs in the park, have produced the most significant changes in the landscape. Active quarrying continues at a number of sites, particularly in the limestone, and its extent is a cause for concern.

About 32,000 people live in the park. The former county town of Brecon, with a population of 7,400, has a long history and many ancient buildings. The park is close to the densely populated areas of South Wales; it is visited by about seven million visitors a year, about two thirds of them day visitors. On the other hand a large number stay in the park, including those who stay at the 100 or more outdoor activity centres. Recreation takes many forms. Walking is very popular and the routes vary from the tow path of the Monmouthshire and Brecon canal (the only canal lying almost wholly within a national park) and disused railway lines, to high level paths among the mountains. Exploration of the caves and underground passages is a challenging sport for the dedicated.

Management

The National Park Authority is active over the whole range of park functions. An important feature is the preparation of a Landscape Strategy Map which will be used to give broad guidance on priorities. Land will be divided into three categories where the preference will be for: semi-natural, broadleaf woodlands or adaptable. The potential for recreation in different parts of the park has been assessed.

The National Park Authority has purchased 8,700 ha of common land. It has initiated more than 50 woodland management schemes and planted more than 400,000 trees in order to retain the characteristic appearance of the landscape. About 20 sites of high ecological value, which were in danger, such as flower-rich and wet meadows, have been safeguarded by informal management agreements. Visitor services cater for hundreds of thousands each year; these are designed to increase the public's understanding of the park and their appreciation of its value. Matters for immediate concern are: the changing pattern of upland agriculture; the need to improve public paths and access to and within the park; improving liaison with educational groups and with the local community; and the conservation of archaeological features and buildings.

Management plans:
>   National Park Plan First Review 1987.

Land ownership:
>   Most in private ownership; 30 per cent is open moorland with commoners' rights. The National Park Authority holds 8,700 ha of common land. Other public bodies (including National Trust, NCC, Forestry Commission and Water Authority) own 17 per cent.

Natural areas of special interest:
>   National Nature Reserves: 4 (783 ha)
>   Other nature reserves: 3 local nature reserves (218 ha) and 17 others
>   Sites of Special Scientific Interest: 44 (27,135 ha)
>   Areas of international importance: caves of the Ogof Ffynnon Ddu complex which are the second longest and the deepest known in Britain.

The built environment:
>   Conservation areas: 3
>   Listed buildings: 829 of many periods

Historic sites and landscapes:
>   Archaeological sites: several hundred are known; 130 have statutory protection as ancient monuments of which 4 are in the direct care of Cadw, Welsh Historic Monuments. Carn Goch near Llangadog is the largest Iron Age fort in Wales, with over 12 ha enclosed in stone banks.

Administering authority:
Brecon Beacons National Park Authority,
7 Glamorgan Street,
Brecon,
Powys LD3 7DP
Tel: (0874) 4437

Dartmoor National Park

Designated 1951   945 sq km

Description

Dartmoor National Park lies in the county of Devon in the south west of England between Exeter to the east and Plymouth to the west. It is the largest and wildest open space in southern England. The core of the park is an upland of granite, much of it standing at over a thousand feet. Two blocks in the north west and south, separated by the River Dart and its tributaries, extend over 460 sq km and consist of smooth contoured hills and wide expanses of bog. Tors, where the granite has weathered into rugged shapes, cap many of the hills. The highest of these are High Willhays (621 m) and Yes Tor (618 m). The land in the north east is at a lower altitude and merges into the farmland of lowland Devon.

The wildness of the park depends upon the wide expanses of high, unenclosed ground and the changing weather. Mist and cloud frequently shroud the hills and the average annual rainfall is high (2,540 mm). The streams and rivers which rise in the bogs run in wide valleys in their upper reaches; where they leave the moor they pass through bands of harder rocks and cascade down waterfalls and rocky gorges in steep, wooded valleys.

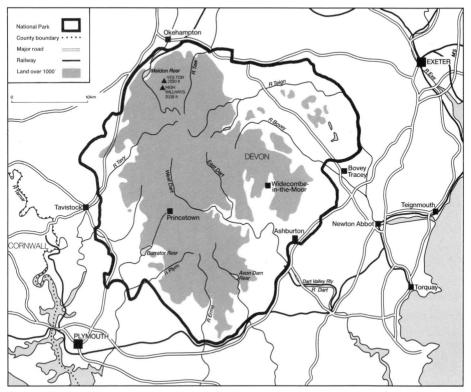

Dartmoor National Park

Granite tors, such as Hound Tor, cap many of the high points of the rolling hills of Dartmoor and add a distinctive character to this western upland.

Stock rearing is the main agricultural use. The small fields enclosed by stone walls, banks and hedges contrast with open, unenclosed moorland. But both are used, for many farmers claim their commoners' rights to graze animals on the open moor. They are the successors to 5,000 years of pastoral agriculture; indeed the park has a unique assembly of early sites and monuments, and complete prehistoric and medieval landscapes have survived.

Tin, copper and iron have all been extracted from the moor and traces of these industries remain, dating from the Iron Age to the twentieth century. The indestructible local granite or moorstone, much used as a building material, has ensured the survival of many ancient monuments and buildings. The park is the best area in England for studying the design and construction of early medieval farmhouses - sometimes all that now remain of the earlier, larger settlements high on the moor.

There are 30,000 residents in the park. Some live in isolated farms, some in moorland villages, but the majority in the villages and small towns that lie in the lower valleys on the fringe of the moor. These, with their attractive stone, slate-hung or colour-washed buildings, many with thatched roofs, are a delightful contrast to the upland settlements. Ashburton was a stannary town, Lydford a centre of administration and Widecombe-in-the-Moor was made wealthy with wool. All owe something to the moor and its granite.

The special character of the Moor makes it a mecca for tourists and the park is visited by some seven to eight million visitors a year.

Management

The passing of the Dartmoor Commons Act in October 1985 was a major achievement. Under this act, the Dartmoor Commoners Council has been constituted for the maintenance and promotion of a proper standard of livestock husbandry on the common lands. It also secures and legalises public access to 364.4 sq km of moorland common which, in conjunction with the 805 km of footpaths and bridleways, does much to promote enjoyment and freedom of movement for pedestrians and horseriders. The National Park Authority has, however, the problem of reconciling this with the military use of large areas of the wildest part of the park.

Although minor concessions have been obtained, an obtrusive military presence remains. The moor is also important as a water catchment area.

The Duchy of Cornwall, which owns 291 sq km of the national park, has developed, in consultation with the National Park Authority, a management plan for its Dartmoor estate which complements and furthers as far as possible the national park purposes in conserving the landscape while pursuing a reasonable economic return.

The Authority has negotiated 36 management agreements. Several are specifically concerned with the integrity of the moorland which is considered to be of paramount importance. They include agreements to bury overhead cables and restrict coniferous plantations. There is also a general voluntary agreement regulating afforestation. In its own woods, the National Park Authority is demonstrating different types of woodland management with the aim of reviving active management of important valley woodlands. There are eight agreements for the protection of archaeological features, but this aspect of conservation is still not satisfactory. Only 430 sites have been scheduled by the Department of the Environment, out of the 6000 or more identified, and only six are under guardianship.

Pressure for more limestone and china clay extraction and for road improvements continues and is difficult to resist where a case is made for them in the national interest. But the procedures introduced in 1980 whereby the National Park Authority is informed of applications for MAFF improvement grants has worked well and a much better understanding has developed between farmers and the Authority. In this climate of improved understanding, the National Park Authority is setting out to achieve sensible arrangements for regulation of grazing and moorland management, and regulating access, legalised in the Dartmoor Commons Act, for the mutual benefit of residents and visitors.

Management plans:
National Park Plan 1977; First Review 1983.
Management plan for the Duchy of Cornwall estates.

Land ownership:
Most of the land is in private ownership. The Duchy of Cornwall is the largest private landowner (29.6 per cent). The National Park Authority owns 1.4 per cent, and other public bodies (National Trust, Forestry Commission, Water Authority, Ministry of Defence and Nature Conservancy Council) about 11 per cent. Forty per cent is common land over which commoners have certain rights, the majority of which belongs to the Duchy.

Natural areas of special interest:
National Nature Reserves: 3 (250 ha)
Other nature reserves: 4 (59 ha)
Sites of Special Scientific Interest: 28 (15,364 ha)

The built environment:
Conservation areas: 17 in villages and small towns. One of these, Ashburton, has also a town scheme involving the Department of the Environment, the National Park Authority and the district council.
Listed buildings: 1750 (being reviewed)
Outstanding large houses and their parks: Castle Drogo (1911-1930)

Historic sites and landscapes:
Archaeological sites: Many monuments of the last 5000 years including the greatest concentration of visible prehistoric remains in north west Europe.

Administering authority:
Dartmoor National Park Authority,
Parke, Haytor Road,
Bovey Tracey,
Newton Abbot,
Devon TQ13 9JQ
Tel: (0626) 832093

Exmoor National Park

Designated 1954   686 sq km

Description

Exmoor National Park lies in the counties of Devon and Somerset in south west England;
Exeter is 40 km to the south and Taunton 20 km from the eastern boundary. The park contains
a wide variety of magnificent landscapes. Despite its comparatively small size, the sweeping
lines of rolling moorland on the central plateau give a great feeling of remoteness and space.
To the north the moorland terminates in towering cliffs above the Bristol Channel. Rocky
headlands, steep wooded ravines, plunging waterfalls and jumbles of fallen rock make this an
area of outstanding scenic beauty; it is proposed as an heritage coast.

Inland the grass moorland, the former royal forest, is surrounded by the heather clad commons;
much of this lies at over 300 m. The whole is dissected by deep combes and contrasts with the
neatly enclosed farmland. Dunkery Beacon, the highest point in the park at 520 m, overlooks
the Brendon Hills to the east. These are heavily wooded in the north but to the south a
landscape of enclosed fields surrounded by banks and fine beech hedges is typical. The land is
mainly farmed with beef cattle and sheep but there is some dairying around the Brendons.

The park is rich in wildlife. There are many different habitats and about 37 per cent is covered
with native plant and animal communities; over 1,800 red deer, the largest British mammal,
roam the moors and woods. The cliffs are the nesting place of a wide variety of sea-birds.
Many of the habitats are small and specialised, and particularly vulnerable to agricultural
improvements such as drainage and to incidental damage from pollution. The ancient
woodlands, mainly coppiced in the past, are composed of native species and are rich in
invertebrates. But the future of some woodlands is threatened by lack of management and
uncontrolled grazing.

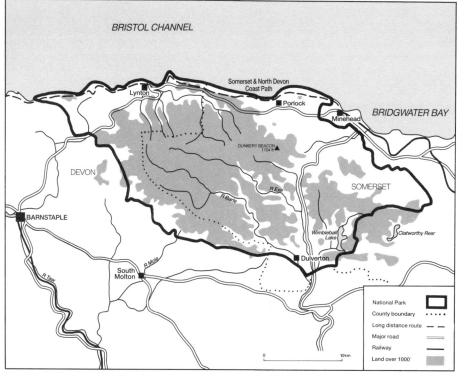

Exmoor National Park

Lynton and Lynmouth, where traditional stone and slate buildings contrast with more ornate Victorian styles, form the largest settlement. In the fertile vale of Porlock, to the east, the villages have cottages of colour washed cob, stone and thatch. Culbone, the smallest parish church in England, commemorates St Beuno, one of the early Celtic missionaries.

Management

The most important concern of management is to retain the remaining areas of moorland. Farming, the traditional land use, has had its share of economic ups and downs. The first half of this century saw a disastrous decline in farm incomes. Since 1945, however, new techniques and MAFF grants have made it possible to "improve" huge areas of moorland. Soils and climate are such that nearly all the park could be improved and increases in income from moorland could be as much as four-fold. By 1968 it was estimated that only 32 per cent of the park could be classified as moorland and heath. Most (21,985 ha) was in the central highland with a few scattered areas elsewhere; of these 16,188 ha (23.5 per cent of the park) were selected as "critical amenity" land. From 1980 onwards these areas have been mapped and the Park Committee has entered into management agreements with the farmers and landowners to ensure the conservation of this valuable landscape. Ninety per cent of the funding for this work came directly from the Department of the Environment. The Committee's pioneering work has become enshrined in the 1981 Wildlife and Countryside Act. The Park Committee has also pioneered grant aid for hedgelaying.

Riding and walking are very popular and public access within the park has been much improved. A comprehensive network of 1200 km of paths has been established with a waymarking system begun in the early 1960s. Forty per cent of the new paths are "permissive", negotiated by the Park Committee with landowners and farmers.

Badgeworthy Water: one of the streams draining the upland of Exmoor. Rounded coombes amid the rolling moorland give way to wooded valleys with clear streams and small rivers. Those draining northwards into the Bristol channel fall steeply to the sea in fine rocky gorges.

Changing economics have led to loss of jobs, particularly in agriculture. Exmoor was the first national park to establish a tourism development action programme. Now 1,000 more people are employed, full-time, in the tourist industry than in agriculture.

Management plans:
> Exmoor National Park Plan. 1977. (Being reviewed in parts.)
> Policies for Park in Structure Plans of Somerset and Devon County Councils.
> A number of local plans.

Land ownership:
> Most in private ownership. About 66 per cent of the coast line publicly owned (National Park Authority 13 per cent; National Trust 49 per cent; other local authorities 4 per cent).

Natural areas of special interest:
> National Nature Reserves: none
> Other nature reserves: 2
> Sites of Special Scientific Interest: 6

The built environment:
> Conservation areas: 8
> Listed buildings: 580.

Historic sites and landscapes:
> Archaeological sites: remains of many periods; the Longstone near Challacombe; Bronze Age stone rows and burials mounds; Iron Age forts.
> Other: relics of 19th century mining; field patterns of the enclosures of the 17th, 18th and 19th centuries.

Administering authority:
> Exmoor National Park Committee (Somerset County Council),
> Exmoor House,
> Dulverton,
> Somerset TA22 9HL
> Tel: (0398) 23665

Lake District National Park

Designated 1951   2280 sq km

Description

The Lake District is situated in the north west of England in the county of Cumbria west of a line between Carlisle to the north and Lancaster to the south. It is the largest of the national parks and forms a natural geographical and cultural unit. It is a land of contrasts; tranquil lakes reflecting the everchanging skies, rugged peaks glimpsed through swirling clouds or pastoral landscapes with stone-walled fields, scattered trees and sturdy farmsteads below the open fells.

Recognition of the exceptional qualities of Lakeland came early. Tourists, some no doubt encouraged by a series of excellent guidebooks, have come to admire the scenery and refresh the spirit for over two centuries. The area has inspired painters and poets and their work has enthused millions both far and near. This very particular admiration and affection has generated much care and concern for the area, especially when changes were threatening. It was here that Wordsworth wrote of "a sort of national property" and here that the National Trust for England and Wales came into being and where it has gone from strength to strength, now owning nearly a quarter of the park.

The Ordovician and Silurian rocks which form the core of the park are over 400 million years

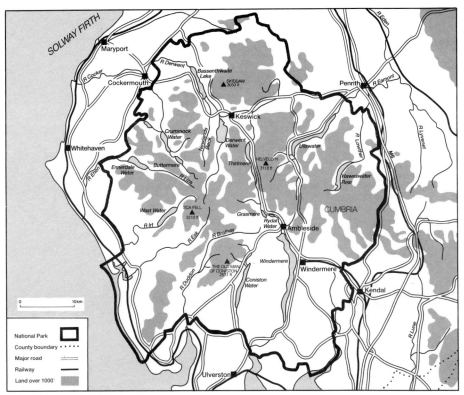

Lake District National Park

old and during their long history have been greatly altered by massive earth movements and the welling up of igneous material.

Now they stand as a dome surrounded by younger sandstones and limestones. Glaciers have sculptured these rocks. The hardest and most resistant at the centre - the Borrowdale Volcanics - stand out as dramatic peaks; among them Helvellyn (950 m) and Scafell Pike (978 m), the highest mountain in England. The Skiddaw Slates in the north form bold, wide-horizoned hills reaching up to 931 m on Skiddaw and the softer Silurian Slates in the south remain as rounded hills amid more gentle scenery. Several valleys radiate out from the central dome, each valley with one or more lakes, 16 in all. These are the jewels of the Lake District and they vary greatly in character: the great stretch of water that is Windermere, the remote and scree-girt Wastwater or the domestic charm of Grasmere.

Man has been using the park for over 5,000 years and has left many traces on the landscape from the great stone circle of Castlerigg near Keswick to the bobbin mills at Stott Park; from the Neolithic axe factories in Langdale to the mineral workings and stone quarries found throughout the hills. For most of the period the area has been used mainly for stock rearing and wool production although in earlier times the valley floors were cultivated. Traces of Iron Age fields can be seen in Upper Langdale and at Blindcrake a wealth of early fields survive. After the Norman conquest several monasteries had sheep walks in the area of the park; the remains of two, Shap and Calder, are scheduled monuments. The fine turf, close cropped by generations of sheep, is one of the delights of the fell walker. Except for the high tops most of the scenery has been strongly influenced by man and the continuance of these landscapes depends on properous farming.

The park covers land from sea level to 978 m. There is a wide variety of habitats, many of great ecological importance nationally - there are 79 SSSI - and internationally. Esthwaite North Fen is a Ramsar site and has been studied for nearly 150 years. The Borrowdale woods are internationally important for their unusual number of oceanic bryophytes.

25

Man's traditional and harmonious use of the landscape is epitomised in this view of Troutbeck in the Lake District. Local stone has been used for the farm buildings and dwelling houses, indigenous, broadleaved trees grow in the hedgerows and semi-natural vegetation provides rough grazing on the fells.

Management

Reconciling the needs of about 40,000 inhabitants, 12 million visitors and the conservation of the landscapes of the park is a continuing exercise. The most popular informal outdoor activity is walking, especially on the fells. The Park Authority pioneered the Upland Management Service and this has been going for over a decade. The service helps to repair and build walls, restores paths and provides guidance and information for the visitors and does much to foster good relations between those who work in the park and those who come for recreation. Brockhole, the main visitor centre, in a fine mansion on the shores of Lake Windermere, caters for all tastes and helps the tourists to enjoy their visits to the full.

The use of the lakes is a matter of concern. Windermere is the only lake where powered boats can travel at more than ten mph and there are by-laws governing the use of many of the lakes. Some have already been used as reservoirs and demand continues; this is one of the matters where a balance has to be struck between the integrity of the park and the national interest.

Many of the most attractive semi-natural communities depend on traditional farming methods. These produced a mixture of hay meadows and grazing interspersed with patches of deciduous woodland and small areas of wetland. Intensification threatens these rich communities of plants and animals. The Park Authority has purchased some broadleaved woodlands and entered into agreements for the management of meadows and wetlands.

The farmsteads, villages and small towns of the park are an important part of its attraction. There are many very interesting vernacular buildings and the Authority has made 14 conservation areas. The two towns of Keswick and Bowness/Windermere are particularly important for tourism. Pressures for further tourist development are continuous and a careful balance has to be maintained between provision for the tourist industry - Cumbria as whole earns £150 million every year from tourism—work for the resident population and maintaining the charm and beauty of the park.

Management plans:
> Lake District National Park Plan First Review 1986.
> (Supplemented by: Joint Management Plan for Haweswater; Windermere Management Plan; and Bassenthwaite Management Plan.)

Land ownership:
> 41.3 per cent publicly owned including the most significant parts for conservation. National Park Authority 3.05 per cent; National Trust 24.38 per cent (22.7 per cent owned, remainder under covenant); Forestry Commission 4.02 per cent; North West Water 5.81 per cent. Rest privately owned.

Natural areas of special interest:
> National Nature Reserves: 4
> Other nature reserves: 13
> Sites of Special Scientific Interest: 79 (14.2 per cent of park)
> Areas of international importance: The park has been proposed as a World Heritage Site; Esthwaite Water is a Ramsar Site; Borrowdale woods are of international importance for their oceanic flora; the area contains one of the highest breeding densities of peregrine falcons in the world.

The built environment:
> Conservation areas: 14, including villages and parts of small towns;
> Listed buildings: 1179 (being reviewed) including 27 of Grade 1 and many examples of vernacular farm and village buildings.

Historic sites and landscapes:
> Archaeological sites: 150 scheduled monuments (being reviewed); the Langdale Neolithic axe factories; traces of traditional field patterns of all periods.
> Others: industrial monuments of mining and water-powered mills; mansions of wealthy industrialists and their parks provide a pastoral landscape with trees around the lakes.

Administering authority:
> Lake District National Park Authority,
> Busher Walk,
> Kendal,
> Cumbria LA9 4RH
> Tel: (0539) 24555

Northumberland National Park

Designated 1956   1,031 sq km

Description

Northumberland National Park is in the extreme north of England in the county of Northumberland, with Carlisle to the south west and Newcastle upon Tyne to the south east. Its northern limit is the crest of the Cheviot Hills on the Scottish border; its southern boundary lies south of the dramatic whinstone sill along which runs Hadrian's Wall, built in AD 120 to defend the northern bounds of the Roman empire. Its wild, rolling hills and upland valleys are frontier country, seeing centuries of conflict between the Romans and the Celtic tribes, and later between the Scots and English. The Wall, castles and fortified houses all bear witness to this turbulent past.

The area is now sparsely inhabited, open country, the domain of the sheep and the walker - the resident population is only 2,500. But there is plenty of internal variety. In the north, the Cheviot Hills rise to 815 m, rolling hills of volcanic rocks covered by wide expanses of grassland and moor, whose delicate colouring and wide skies give a tremendous impression of space. Secluded valleys radiate from the centre with crags and small woods of birch, rowan and oak. The Simonside Hills and Harbottle Hills, in the middle of the park, are formed of sandstones and other sedimentary rocks and are in sharp contrast, being mainly covered with heather. To the south, substantial areas are afforested, part of the Border Forest which lies mainly outside the park to the west, and is the largest expanse of man-made forest in Britain. The country of the Roman Wall has a character all of its own. Between these blocks of upland run the valleys of the Rede and the North Tyne with their stone-built farms, meadow pastures and shelter belts of trees. The waters of the North Tyne are impounded by the Kielder Water reservoir (a lake as large as Ullswater in the Lake District), which is situated on the edge of the national park.

The land in the park is privately owned except for one-fifth which is a training area for the Ministry of Defence, inherited from the days before the park was established, and one-fifth which belongs to the Forestry Commission. Apart from the forest, this is a land of sheep. The special character of the landscape and the pattern of settlement both depend upon the continued prosperity of the sheep farmer. The future of upland agriculture is therefore the main worry for the Park Authority.

Management

The area of the park around Hadrian's Wall, an historic monument with an international reputation, and the unpopulated hills of Cheviot are very different in character, posing different problems which require different solutions. Provision of recreational facilities and

The Cheviot, and the Cheviot hills in general, form the northern boundary of the Northumberland National Park on the Scottish border. This sparsely populated country is a land of sheep; the long distance walker, for instance on the northern stretches of the Pennine Way, crosses landscapes of immense space and emptiness.

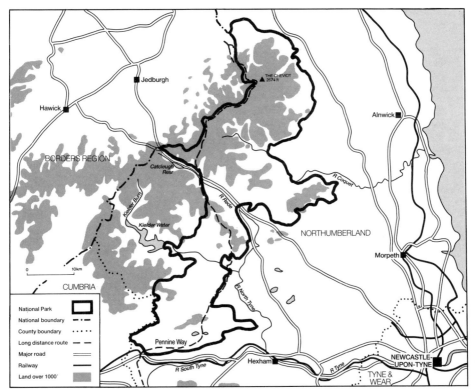

Northumberland National Park

easing the lot of the landowners and farmers in the south are all-important; this includes agreements with the National Trust on the management, wardening and information services on the Housesteads estate, one of the most popular stretches of the Wall.

About one million visit the park each year, half of these from Tyneside. Access for the public on the hills is legally restricted to the footpaths and rights of way. The National Park Authority has initiated access in some areas (the park includes 105 km of the Pennine Way) and also has a wide range of guided walks appealing to varying abilities and interests which greatly enhance people's enjoyment of the park.

Long before the park came into being large areas were being used for military training and forestry and these uses cause problems. Access to the firing range at Otterburn is restricted but there is cooperation with the Ministry of Defence in improving the appearance of existing facilities and in limiting further developments. The Forestry Commission plantations, mainly of conifers, are considered by many to be an intrusive element in the open landscape. The Park Authority has an agreement which limits the siting and scale of any new planting, and through consultation can influence the management of existing forests. In addition, the Commission has opened many drives and waymarked walks within their forests for the benefit of the public. The Park Authority has also initiated a substantial programme for bringing semi-natural woodland under management and is helping landowners, farmers and visitors by its Upland Management Works Programme.

The most persistent and pressing issue, as in many of the other parks, is the changing structure of upland agriculture. The conservation of many elements of the landscape is dependent upon a satisfactory economic base for rural land use. Other changing national needs and new enterprises bring fresh and unexpected problems such as the possible disposal of radio-active waste in the Cheviots or the exploitation of coal deposits in the south of the park.

Management plans:
   National Park Plan 1977. First review, 1984; second due in 1989.

Land ownership:
   20 per cent Ministry of Defence; 20 per cent Forestry Commission; remainder private; small areas Park Authority.

Natural areas of special interest:
   National Nature Reserves: 2
   Other nature reserves: 2 Local Nature Reserves; 18 Wildlife Trust reserves.
   Sites of Special Scientific Interest: 20, including 2 of >4,000 ha
   Areas of international importance: the Irthinghead Mires are a Ramsar site.

The built environment:
   Conservation areas: Nil
   Listed buildings: 51 (being reviewed)

Historic sites and landscapes:
   Archaeological sites: 170 scheduled monuments, including stretches of Hadrian's Wall and associated Roman features. Some significant areas still to be scheduled. Many Iron Age hillforts, Yeavering Bell the largest.
   Other: the convergence of ancient drove roads from Scotland; sites of several deserted villages with their old ridge and furrow lines; stone-walled sheep pens (stells), a feature of the Cheviot valleys.

Administering authority:
   National Park and Countryside Committee,
   (Northumberland County Council),
   Eastburn, South Park,
   Hexham,
   Northumberland NE46 1BS
   Tel: (0434) 605555

North York Moors National Park

Designated 1952   1,432 sq km

Description

The North York Moors National Park lies in north-east England at the junction of the counties of North Yorkshire and Cleveland. The rich agricultural Vale of York is to the south and to the north the heavily industrialised areas of Teeside and Tyneside. The heather-covered hills of the park, which rise to heights up to 454 m, stand out clearly from the flat surrounding vales. From the roads, which follow the ridges, there are breathtaking views across the undulating hills and down the deeply incised dales where farmland and woods surround abbeys, castles and small villages. High rugged cliffs above the North Sea form the eastern boundary where there are attractive fishing villages such as Robin Hood's Bay and Staithes with steep streets leading to minute harbours. This is a defined heritage coast.

The park is an uplifted plateau of Jurassic rocks forming a series of scarps, most of which face north, composed of limestones, sandstones, gritstones, shales and clays. A number of small rivers drain southwards down the dip slope forming beautiful, wooded dales that cut through the Tabular Hills between Helmsley and Pickering. Mineral deposits such as iron stone, alum and coal occur throughout the park and have been exploited in the past, the iron for 2,000 years; the last mine closed in 1964. But further exploitation of some minerals, especially potash, remains a threat.

The ruins of Rievaulx Abbey stand as a reminder that man has shaped the landscape of Britain for millenia. The land use of the monastic foundations from the Conquest to the Dissolution, especially their huge flocks of sheep, have had a profound effect on the uplands.

The park contains one of the finest assemblages of archaeological sites in Britain, ranging from the Palaeolithic to the recent industrial past. From 3500 BC mixed farming was carried on in the Hambleton and Tabular Hills and there are remains of rudimentary field enclosures from Neolithic times. Field clearance and deliberate burning to provide grazing began in the Mesolithic and continued throughout the Bronze Age with accelerating podsolisation of the soils. The boundaries of the small scale settlements of this period survive as the parish boundaries of today. Many landscape features from the Iron Age also remain: large linear earthworks, field patterns, house and defensive sites and remains of smelting works. A fine Roman road can still be seen on Wheeldale Moor and there is a unique group of military practice camps near Pickering. Forty medieval crosses are found on the moor and the religious foundations of the period, such as the magnificent Rievaulx monastery, have left their legacy. The Whitby-Pickering Railway, constructed by George Stephenson, still runs through a spectacular and roadless landscape of gorges and remote valleys.

There is a wide range of habitats and 68 per cent of the park is of high ecological value. About one third is covered with moorland and upland heaths and some 60 per cent of this has some form of protection. These heaths are managed for sheep and red grouse and are the nesting place of the merlin. Unusually, they have developed over young rocks in an area of relatively low rainfall (760 mm generally, 1000 mm on high moors), probably as a result of early man's activities. There are now substantial areas of peat which are vulnerable to fire during drought.

Mixed deciduous woodlands cover five per cent of the park and are of considerable variety depending on the type of soil. Many have rich plant communities including a number of rarities. The wooded ravines along the coast are valuable resting places for many migratory birds. These species-rich woodlands contrast strongly with the 20 per cent of the park which is covered with forestry plantations. The remaining 40 per cent of the area is farmland and

31

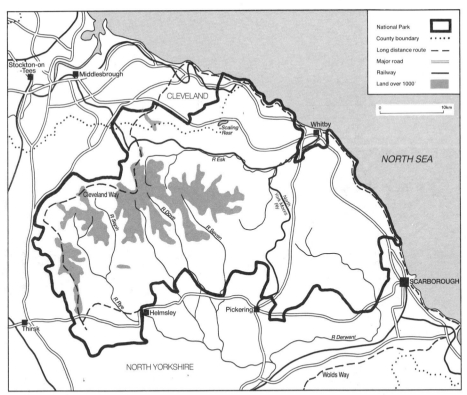

North York Moors National Park

within this there are many sites of great ecological and aesthetic value such as damp hay meadows, daffodil fields and limestone grassland.

There are 1,818 km of public rights of way. The public has traditional, but no formal, access to the open moorland. There are 16 regionally and nationally known long distance paths in the park, the best known being the Cleveland Way (150 km) around the boundaries, and the Lyke Wake Walk, an east-west route of 67 km.

Lying as it does within a short distance of highly urbanised areas the park is visited by many people - 11 million visits in a year and as many as 137,000 visitors on a fine Sunday afternoon.

Management

Agriculture is the main land use, taking up 48 per cent of the park, including some enclosed moorland. Without thriving agriculture the landscape and social fabric (25,000 people live in the park) would decline; but intensification can destroy the character of the area. The loss of heather moorland, 155 sq km since 1950, has had a major effect. The Park Committee have initiated a moorland management programme to improve the state and future prospects of the moor. They have also purchased Lockton High Moor to demonstrate moorland conservation techniques. Complementing this programme, the Committee carries out upland management schemes to assist farmers to maintain landscape features and to repair and restore those that have deteriorated from lack of labour or have been damaged by overuse.

Sixty per cent of the broadleaved woodlands are less than four ha in size and are showing little sign of regeneration. If this deterioration continues, sites will be lost that are valuable for animal husbandry - over wintering stock, and for intrinsic ecological interest. The Committee has begun several Woodland Management and Tree Planting Schemes. In 1983/4, 7544 trees were planted. They have also acquired Levisham Woods as a demonstration area for the conservation of woodland.

Ten management agreeements for the conservation of areas of high nature conservation interest are in operation, most of these on farmland and the Committeee has also initiated a number of Farm Conservation Plans.

Being on the eastern seaboard the park is required, in the national interest, to play a part in the Fylingdales Ballistic Missiles Early Warning System.

Management plans:
    National Park Plan 1977; First Review 1894; Management Plan for the Bransdale Moor estate (6237 ha, much an SSSI) accepted in lieu of Capital Transfer Tax.

Land ownership:
    Most of the land is in private ownership. National Park Authority 2 per cent; National Trust c 1 per cent; water authorities 4 per cent; Forestry Commission 16.5 per cent. Of the protected moorland 49.4 per cent is common land; 12.1 per cent is covered by Capital Transfer Tax exemption and the National Park Committee owns 1.6 per cent.

Natural areas of special interest:
    National Nature Reserves: 3
    Other nature reserves: 1 Local Nature Reserve (Farndale >1000 ha); 8 Yorkshire Wildlife
        Trust
    Sites of Special Scientific Interest: 40

The built environment:
    Conservation areas: 18. There are town schemes in Staithes and Robin Hood's Bay.
    Listed buildings: 800 (being resurveyed)

Historic sites and landscapes:
    Archaeological sites: 300 scheduled ancient monuments; there are also many areas of
        special archaeological significance, prehistoric, Roman and medieval; four are under
        the guardianship of English Heritage.

Administering authority:
    North York Moors National Park Committee,
    North Yorkshire County Council,
    The Old Vicarage,
    Bondgate, Helmsley,
    York YO6 5BP
    Tel: (0439) 70657

Peak National Park

Designated 1951   1,404 sq km

Description

The first established of the National Parks, the Peak lies at the southern end of the Pennines. The road between Huddersfield and Oldham crosses the northern tip of the park, the city of Sheffield reaches its eastern boundary and the conurbation of Manchester lies to the west; Nottingham, Derby and the Potteries are within 30 km of its southern border. In short, the Peak National Park lies at the centre of the old industrial heart of England and about a third of the population of the country lives within 80 km of its borders and is easily able to reach this magnificent open space with its two very contrasting landscapes - the Dark Peak with its imposing escarpments and wild sepia moors of the high hills and the softer, greener plateau of the White Peak.

Millstone Grit dominates the scenery of much of the Dark Peak. Wide valleys slope up to open moorlands of grass, heather or bog. More dramatic scenery appears where 'edges' or escarpments such as Curbar Edge, near Bakewell, break the smooth contours. Dry stone walls are an important part of the landscape.

The rocks of the park belong to the Carboniferous series which have been raised into a dome by later earth movements. The core of the southern part is a great mass of limestones of different ages and characteristics. A band of shales surrounds the limestone and separates it from the Millstone Grit which bounds the park on the east and west and dominates the north, Here most of the land is above 300 m and rises from steep valleys and wide expanses of moor and bog to hills such as Bleaklow (628 m) and Kinder Scout (636 m). To the south, the limestone forms an extensive plateau at about 300 m which is abruptly and deeply incised by narrow, steep-sided dales; miniature canyons, buttresses and isolated pinnacles are part of the scenery.

The vegetation of the park reflects the underlying differences in the rock. Vast areas of Millstone Grit, much of it peat covered, carry heather on the better drained soils with cotton grass moors and bogs on the wetter ground. Remnants of the native birch and oak woods survive in steep valleys but are rare, contrasting with the dark spreads of recent conifer plantations. The grasslands of the limestone plateau and the dales are very rich in species. Native woodlands have long disappeared from the upland but shelter belts and hilltop clumps are a characteristic landscape feature. Fine examples of native woodland with many species are found in the dales and rare plants are found on ledges inaccessible to grazing animals. A number of species of bat, now all protected, roost in some of the limestone caves.

Early man has left many signs of his presence in the park. A Bronze Age landscape is found at Big Moor and numerous "lows" mark the burial tumuli of this civilisation. Mam Tor near Castleton is one of several Iron Age hilltop forts and Celtic field systems remain at Blackwell near Taddington. Both limestone and gritstone have been quarried for centuries and used for all types of building. The park has a number of fine houses and parks, the best known being Chatsworth, built of the local gritstone. with its grounds laid out and the River Derwent tamed by "Capability" Brown.

Many minerals are found in the park. For 2,000 years lead has been mined and this has left traces in the limestone area both in place names and on the ground. The undulating grasslands of the plateau have smaller scale irregularities where the miners dug the veins of lead, called "rakes". Around lead mining villages such as Bradwell there are tiny, stone-walled fields used by the miners to protect their farm animals from the dangers of lead-poisoned grazing. Lead-mine shafts remain as monuments to the era and many villages still have a mining character.

Management

Quarrying remains an important use of the land and one which exercises the Park Board considerably. The boundaries of the park were drawn to exclude the heavily quarried area around Buxton but Eldon Hill and Topley Pike, among others, are both active quarries within the park. During 1985/86 the Park Board had to make its case against extensions to these quarries at lengthy public enquiries and the Secretary of State upheld the Board's case at both.

Exploitation of other minerals including fluorspar continues. The Board has to be vigilant to reconcile the landscape integrity of the park with the national interest in these minerals.

The well-being of the communities in the park depends upon steady employment and those in upland areas were among the first to suffer from the recession. The Park Board, in association with several other bodies, has been carrying out an Integrated Rural Development scheme, originally sponsored by the European Community, in Longnor and Monyash. Two of the conclusions are that social, economic and environmental interests should be considered together for a successful rural policy and that the management and development of attractive landscapes and villages depend crucially on the willing involvement of those who live and work there.

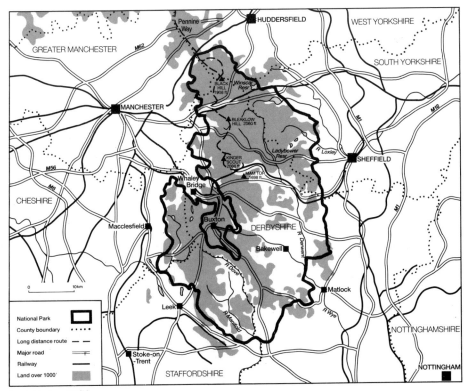

Peak National Park

35

A re-survey of the buildings of the park has indicated that there are over 2,000 worthy of listing and that of these seven per cent are in urgent need of repair. Sometimes the best means of restoration is to turn the building to a new use; many of the beautiful old stone barns are now no longer needed for agricultural work and the Peak Park has pioneered the use of these as "stone tents" - cheap, simple and dry accommodation for walkers.

The Board has entered into management agreements with many farmers to safeguard a variety of sites including flower-rich meadows, wetlands and woodlands. In 1985 the Ministry of Agriculture introduced a new grant scheme which offers grants for a number of activities, some of which are directly for environmental improvement. The consultations between the farmers and the Park Board before the grant is approved have been very valuable.

Reconciling the continuity of woodland with legitimate commercial forestry calls for close cooperation between the landowner, the Forestry Commission and the Park Board. After lengthy discussions this has recently been achieved with the Chatsworth estate for felling and replanting in sensitive areas.

The Peak Park Board has for many years pioneered new ways of dealing with large numbers of visitors. This remains a problem, particularly in the very popular places such as Dovedale, Castleton and the Pennine Way, which starts in the park. Losehill Hall, the park's study centre, and the other information centres help visitors to learn about the park and its value. Traffic management schemes such as those in the Goyt and Upper Derwent valleys and the opening of the "Routes for People" in the White Peak enable the public to enjoy the park free from traffic.

The Peak District National Park was, in 1966, the first area to receive the European Diploma of the Council of Europe.

Management plans:
   National Park Plan 1978; First Review 1987.
   Management plans for: Longdendale, Dovestone, Macclesfield Forest and Wildboarclough, Upper Derwent Valley, Eastern Moors, Roaches, North Lees and Warslow Moors.

Land ownership:
   Most of the land is in private ownership. Water authorities own 1.5 per cent; the Peak Park Board owns 4 per cent; the National Trust owns 10 per cent.

Natural areas of special interest:
   National Nature Reserves: 1 (262 ha).
   Other nature reserves: no number available
   Sites of Special Scientific Interest: 55
   Areas of international importance: the limestone dales and Kinder-Bleaklow plateau.

The built environment:
   Conservation areas: 23 in villages and small towns.
   Listed buildings: c 2200 (expected to rise to 2500 by 1988)
   Outstanding large houses and their parks: Many including Chatsworth, Haddon Hall, Lyme Hall, and several around Hathersage.

Historic sites and landscapes:
   Archaeological sites: many scheduled ancient monumemts, including Big Moor and Arbor Low (in the guardianship of English Heritage) and Mam Tor.
   Others: Saxon crosses; many remains of lead mining including Magpie Mine, Tideslow Rake, Oxlow Rake, Lathkill Dale; Winster village and surroundings; early waterpowered cotton mills including Cressbrook.

Administering authority:
   The Peak Park Joint Planning Board,
   Aldern House, Baslow Road,
   Bakewell,
   Derbyshire DE4 1AE
   Tel: (062 981) 4321

Pembrokeshire Coast National Park

Designated 1952   583 sq km

Description

The Pembrokeshire Coast National Park takes the form of coastal strips and islands around the south-west peninsula of Wales in the county of Dyfed. The presence of the sea permeates everywhere and the magnificent cliffs and attractive bays, the brilliant sheets of flowers along the cliff tops and hedgerows, the mild sunny climate and the rolling Preseli hills - so much a part of Welsh prehistory and folk-lore - give the park a very particular quality.

The ages of the rocks in the park cover an immensely wide span of geological time - from the pre-Cambrian near St David's to the Carboniferous in the south. The imprint of many ancient earth movements can be seen in the rocks but two of the most important elements of the present day landscape are due to fluctuations in the relative levels of sea and land during the last few million years. These are the great sinuous inlet of Milford Haven which owes its appearance to the drowning of the lower parts of ancient river valleys (rias), and the remarkably level plateau at about 60 m above the sea - a wave-cut platform, exposed by a drop in sea level, which now forms much of the peninsula. There are a few exceptions to this uniform horizon; the most notable being the Preseli Hills which rise to a height of 543 m on Foel Cwmcerwyn.

Much of the wildness and open space of the Pembrokeshire Coast National Park is found in its dramatic, rocky coastline and offshore islands. Ramsey Sound, a narrow channel with treacherous currents, separates Ramsey Island from the mainland. Walkers can enjoy the natural beauty and wildlife of the area along the Pembrokeshire Coast Path.

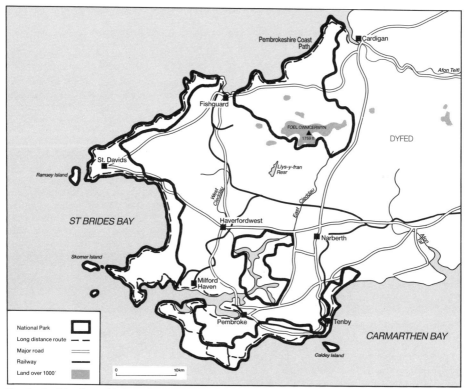

Pembrokeshire Coast National Park

Although there is much windy weather and a fairly low rainfall (average 787 mm) the climate is equable, frost infrequent and the growing season long. There is much sunshine and the park is a pleasant place to live in. The climate and the fertile soils support intensive arable farming along the coast; the early potato crop is well known. Dairying predominates inland and sheep on the Preseli Hills.

There is a rich and varied flora from the heather moorland and bogs of Preseli to the sheets of western gorse and the wealth of flowers along the cliff tops and in the sheltered hedgerows and lanes of the farmland. Saltmarshes, sand dunes and cliffs increase the variety of habitat. There are some rarities but it is the profusion of many kinds of common flowers which is the especial joy. The cliffs of the mainland and islands are famed nesting sites for many thousands of sea birds - puffins, guillemots, razorbills, Manx shearwaters, storm petrels, fulmars, gannets and all the British gulls. The rare chough breeds in several places. Grey seals have their largest breeding colony in Wales on Ramsey. Many migratory birds also visit the coast and the islands.

There is evidence of early man's activities everywhere in the landscape. Limestone caves were occupied 20,000 years ago. Impressive tombs (cromlechs) stand along the cliff tops and on the hills as memorials to the Neolithic inhabitants. Perhaps the most well known activity from this period is the use of doleritic stones from Preseli at Stonehenge, 290 km away on Salisbury Plain. The first Iron Age settlers came to Wales from Gaul 2,500 years ago and have left their legacy of defensive embankments, hilltop forts and stone walled fields some of which are still in use today. The vigour of the monastic movement within the early Christian church has left its mark in the ancient foundation of St David and in the notable group of chapels dedicated to Celtic saints which lie along the coast, mainly at landing places for those on pilgrimage to St David's. The division of Pembrokeshire into the Welsh north and the English south is directly attributable to the Norman occupation of south Pembrokeshire in the late 11th century. The ruins of a number of small castles survive along this line but the most impressive castles which remain (such as Pembroke, Carew and Manorbier) were built behind this line; only some of these are within the park. Wiseman's Bridge was the scene of a rehearsal for the 1944 D-Day Normandy landings.

The resident population is 22,000, the most dense of any national park. Tenby, with a population of 5,000, is an historic sea port with much fine architecture - half the listed buildings of the park are in the town. About 1.33 million visitors stay in the park (1984 estimate) for an average of 11 nights; 95 per cent of the visitors come from more than 20 miles away. They bring considerable trade to the area (recent estimates suggest £122 million per year) but pressure for holiday accomodation results in many applications for housing development; the National Park Authority deals with over 600 planning applications every year. Seasonal congestion on some narrow roads and seasonal strain on public and park services are continuing problems.

Management

The National Park Authority has been active in conservation management. It has a number of agreements for the conservation of natural sites, the most numerous being those to conserve moorland from intensification of agricultural use. A Map of Moor and Heath has been prepared; complete cover of air photographs has been commissioned and mapping has been extended to all natural and semi-natural habitats. The Authority has acquired a number of broadleaved woodlands. It has entered into over 20 tree planting agreements and about 5,000 trees are planted each year.

During the Second World War the park was of great strategic importance and contained many war-time airfields. This has left its legacy of derelict sites which the Authority is actively clearing with help from the Welsh Development Agency.

The National Park Authority has recently received powers to establish, control and improve footpaths. Access to the moorland - ten per cent of the park - is traditionally free but elsewhere the needs of farming have priority, so that footpaths are especially important. The Pembrokeshire Coast Path (297 km) is the best known. There is a footpath network of over 650 km in the farmed area and the National Park Authority is just about to open a new 110 km round walk in the less well-known inland Daugleddau sector of the park around the upper reaches of the Milford Haven waterway.

There are seven information centres in the park and an active park interpretive programme of guided walks, talks and tours throughout the year - in all about 400 events including a dramatic presentation in Carew Castle.

The Authority is active in conservation schemes in the towns and villages and has prepared local plans for the park's three main population centres and several informal village plans. There are two important conservation areas, Tenby and St David's, including the cathedral of Wales' patron saint and the bishop's palace. Both areas are "outstanding".

The Authority runs a National Park Conservation Awards Scheme.

Management plans:
    National Park Plan 1977; Reviewed every 5 years.

Land ownership:
    Most of the land is in private ownership. The National Park Authority owns 0.5 per cent; the National Trust owns 4.7 per cent including about 30 per cent of the coastline; Forestry Commission 1.2 per cent; Ministry of Defence 4.5 per cent; Nature Conservancy Council 0.5 per cent; other public bodies 0.6 per cent.

Natural areas of special interest.
    National Nature Reserves: 3
        Proposed Skomer Island Marine Nature Reserve.
    Other Nature Reserves: 21
    Sites of Special Scientific Interest: 48 (7700 ha)
    Areas of international importance: Most of the islands and many cliff habitats and their adjacent waters.

The built environment:
>   Conservation areas: 2 and one where the park boundary bisects a village.
>   Listed buildings: 800 including St David's cathedral and bishop's palace, and Carew and
>   Manorbier castles.
>   Tenby and Newport both medieval planned towns; Tenby town walls intact.

Scheduled ancient monuments: 200 (similar number unscheduled).

Historic sites and landscapes:
>   Archaeological: Skomer Island an Iron Age landscape; Preseli Hills little changed since
>   the Neolithic; Iron Age settlements and field boundaries on St David's Head; many
>   remains of Iron Age promontory and hillforts.
>   Other: Medieval strip fields at Angle; many defensive sites including mid-Victorian
>   examples round Milford Haven.

Administering authority:
>   Pembrokeshire Coast National Park Committee (Dyfed County Council),
>   County Offices,
>   Haverfordwest,
>   Pembrokeshire,
>   Dyfed SA61 1QZ
>   Tel:(0437) 4591

Snowdonia National Park

Designated 1951   2,170 sq km

Description

The Snowdonia National Park stands in the north west of Wales in the county of Gwynedd. Snowdon, the highest mountain in Wales and England, is one of the magnificent assembly of hills which have kept this corner of Wales a cultural and patriotic stronghold for centuries. The language, tradition and culture of the Welsh still flourish. Being close to the sea in the north and west the full splendour of the mountains can be appreciated giving them a stature far in excess of their 1,000 metres.

The rocks of the park began as sediments in Cambrian, Ordovician and Silurian times but they have had a turbulent history of uplift, folding, tilting and compression, interspersed with periods of igneous activity, so that they have been much changed. Slate, once the source of an industry which has left an indelible mark on the landscape, is one of the products of these events. During the last million years glaciers have carved the hardened rocks into rugged mountains, gouged out valleys and lakes, left hanging valleys and waterfalls and deposited moraines. Nine major groups of mountains can be distinguished separated by fine, often wooded, river valleys. Several main roads use the valleys so that even the traveller gets an impression of the wild and mountainous country. The character of the different groups varies from the rocky and precipitous such as Tryfan (917 m), much used for preparatory climbing before ascents of Everest, to the smoother contours of Diffwys and Y Llethr looking out over Cardigan Bay. The summit of Snowdon, Yr Wyddfa Fawr, rises from the junction of five converging ridges, three of them knife edged. From the top magnificent views extend westwards to the sea, and east and south across miles of mountainous country. It is no wonder that to the Welsh it has always been a very special place and is now a magnet for tourists.

Sandy beaches and dunes, estuaries and river meadows, ancient deciduous woodlands, grasslands, moorlands and peat bogs, and the sparse vegetation of the rocky tops and screes are all found in the national park. With over 50 lakes and many smaller pools there is also a great variety of fresh water life. The gwyniad, a small endemic fish, is found in Llyn Tegid (Bala Lake). Much of the vegetation is semi-natural having been shaped by centuries of grazing. Unusually for Britain, goats were one of the principal grazing animals and they are credited with the almost total destruction of the indigenous forest. In 1066 forest covered 60 per cent of the area; 900 years later it was reduced to 3 per cent. Many of the SSSIs and nature reserves are

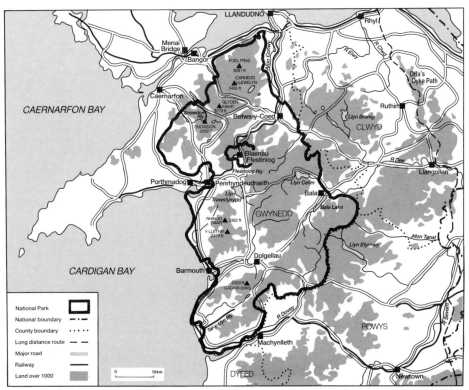

Snowdonia National Park

deciduous woods with their rich assemblages of plants and animals. The Park Committee is doing much to improve their management and plant trees. The Forestry Commission have considerable areas of commercial forest; this was one of the first areas to be planted after the Commission came into being in 1919. Above the tree-line, arctic-alpine vegetation survives in the rigorous climate; here the delicate Snowdon lily, an endemic, is to be found.

Man has left his mark on the landscape for millenia, from the megaliths of the early Neolithic to the slate quarries of the last century. New Stone Age men were the first people to leave evidence of an "industry" in the park; at Craiglwyd, near Penmaenmawr, there is the site of an axe-factory whose products have been found at Stonehenge. For two centuries slate was a boom industry and the tips and abandoned quarries can be seen in many places, sometimes quite wild and remote, although the park boundary has been drawn to exclude the most heavily exploited areas. Buildings, fences and grave stones of slate give a very particular character to some areas such as Llanberis and Harlech.

The Romans and the drovers have left their roads and the sheep farmers their stone walls and enclosures, the Welsh kings and princes their castles, of which perhaps the most romantic is Harlech castle, immortalised by Turner, which Edward I built as part of his girdle of impregnable fortresses surrounding Snowdonia.

Management

The first recorded tourist, an Englishman, climbed Snowdon in 1639. The latest figures suggest that around 300,000 now make the ascent each year; between 200,000 and 250,000 on foot, the rest on the railway. There are six well defined paths up the mountain and by the 1970s all were showing signs of excessive wear and tear. Also the buildings on the summit, which were privately owned, had reached a state of considerable disrepair. After obtaining consultants' advice the Countryside Commission for England and Wales gave special funds of over £1/2

Snowdonia's wild mountain tops contrast with gentle valley landscapes, many with fine woodlands such as these along the Watkin Path. Most of the woods are of great age and many are SSSIs. The National Park Committee is doing much to improve the management of the woodlands and ensure their continuity. Similar schemes are being undertaken in all the national parks.

million to the National Park Authority to rebuild the structures on the summit and restore and reinforce the footpaths. A ground staff of 12 and three wardens cope with the crowds of visitors. Restoration of footpaths is a constant task and one in which the Authority is becoming very skilful.

The main use of the land is for stock farming, principally of sheep. The farms were small but amalgamations have taken place and the agricultural work force is much reduced. Farmhouses in more remote areas have been deserted or taken over as second homes. Tourism is becoming the dominant industry of the area; very many people pass through or visit the park (probably of the order of nine million visitor days). On the other hand, rural depopulation continues and support is needed for local communities through the creation of further jobs and maintenance of services.

After an experimental period in the early 1970s the National Park Committee agreed in 1977 to establish a permanent upland management service. This works both for the benefit of farmers, by assisting them in their care of landscape features, and of visitors.

Better roads to the park continue to lead to great increases in the number of visitors. There is a visitor centre at Betws-y-Coed, a residential study centre at Plas Tan-y-Bwlch and five other visitor information centres run by the National Park Authority; these add to enjoyment and understanding of the park and all it contains.

Low-flying aircraft destroy any feeling of remoteness and peace; in this instance the training of pilots for the defence of the realm conflicts with the quality of the park.

Management plans:
National Park Plan 1977; First Review 1987; Plan for Snowdon Management Area; Structure Plan; 6 local plans, one in preparation.

Land ownership:
Most of the land is in private ownership; National Park Authority 0.5 per cent; the National Trust owns 20,000 ha in Gwynedd, much of it in the National Park; Forestry Commission 16 per cent; Water Authority 6 per cent; common land 11 per cent.

Natural areas of special interest:
National Nature Reserves: 16 (6731.9 ha)
Other nature reserves: 1 (36.0 ha)
Sites of Special Scientific Interest: 71 (32490.5 ha)

The built environment:
Conservation areas: 11
Listed buildings: 390
Outstanding large houses and parks: Plas Tan-y-Bwlch.

Historic sites and landscapes:
Archaeological sites: 132 listed; this is estimated to be only 5 per cent of the total; of these 7 are in guardianship.
Other; many remains of slate mining and of gold, copper and lead mining.

Administering authority:
Snowdonia National Park Committee (County of Gwynedd),
Snowdonia National Park Headquarters,
Penrhyndeudraeth,
Gwynedd LL48 6LS
Tel: (0766) 770247

Yorkshire Dales National Park

Designated 1954   1,761 sq km

Description

The Yorkshire Dales National Park lies astride the Pennines in the north of England in the counties of North Yorkshire and Cumbria; there are over 20 main dales, differing much from each other in character and atmosphere. To the south lies a highly populated industrial area - eight million people live within 90 minutes drive of the southern boundary - while to the north thinly settled uplands stretch to the Tees and beyond. About 17,000 people live in the scattered farms, villages and small market towns of the park.

Limestone is at the heart of the Dales country. Impressive inland cliffs at Gordale Scar and Malham Cove; wide stretches of limestone pavement; dramatic gorges and waterfalls; unexpected swallow holes; deep caves, underground rivers and passages; and a landscape of pastoral valleys patterned with drystone walls, field barns and stone-built villages - all derived from the great thickness of Carboniferous Limestone that underlies the park, sometimes at considerable depth. Limestone is again dominant in the terraced landscapes of Wensleydale and Wharfedale where narrower bands are interspersed with shales, sandstones and even some thin seams of coal.

Above the limestone, Millstone Grit caps the fells which attain their greatest heights in the west. Whernside (737 m), Ingleborough (722 m) and Pen-y-ghent (693 m) form a compact group of challenging tops which comprise the popular Three Peaks Walk.

Limestone dominates the Dales country. Limestone pavement is just one of the unusual land forms of this type of rock. Here the deeply fissured rock is exposed in a flat surface which appears to be completely barren but many rare and unusual plants grow in the joints and clefts.

Most of the area lies at over 180 m and the growing season is short. Stock farming is the most important land use, dairying in the dales and sheep farming on the hills. The pattern of settlement was laid down in the centuries between 700 and 1000 AD when Danes and Angles penetrated the dales from the east and established their nucleated villages; and the Norse, coming from the west, founded their isolated farmsteads high up the valleys. After the Norman invasion four centuries of monasticism finally removed the indigenous tree cover from the hills and dales where large flocks of sheep brought wealth to the Church. It was after the Dissolution of the monasteries that yeomen farmers produced the main features of the cultural landscape which is so highly prized today. Many of the dry stone walls, so characteristic of the area, are the result of enclosures carried out between 1760 and 1820. These fields were usually between three and 12 acres. But in a number of places, for example Malham and in Wharfedale, it is possible to contrast these with the older, smaller enclosures round village croft fields. Indeed the history of the landscape can be read in the pattern of its stone walls.

Earlier peoples have left their marks on the landscape - field systems of the Iron Age and earlier, the large Iron Age fort on the summit of Ingleborough and the Roman garrison post at Bainbridge.

Mineral exploitation has been carried on for hundreds of years and some quarrying continues to detract from the landscape. In the past lead was mined extensively, exploitation reaching a peak in the 18th and 19th centuries. Relict landscapes with evocative ruins remain to this day. Some of the tiny hamlets in Arkengarthdale are the scattered homesteads built by the miners as they exploited the ore-bearing ground.

Peat, sometimes to a depth of 9 metres, covers much of the wetter western uplands. The vegetation of these moors has few species and is dominated by heather and grasses with

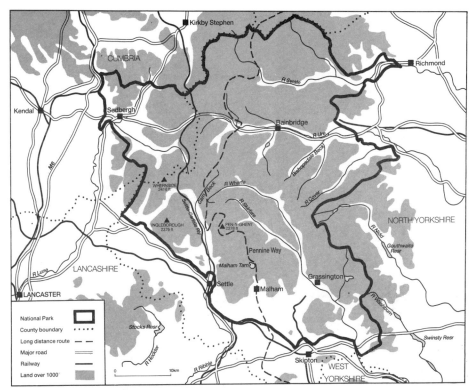

Yorkshire Dales National Park

expanses of cotton grass. Heather also occupies the drier ground between 300 and 425 metres. These upland fells are the home of red grouse and many moorland birds such as curlew, golden plover, merlin and peregrine. The dominant impression of much of the park is of a landscape devoid of trees but remnants of woodland remain in the steep gills and valleys and along the limestone scars. The plant communities of the uplands are composed of few species and are a marked contrast, both in colour and composition, to those of the limestone, whether the dry grasslands dominated by sheep's fescue, the valley floor meadows brilliant with summer flowers or the rich woodlands. For example, a nature reserve in Wharfedale on limestone pavement and scree has a flora of over 400 species.

Management

There are 1,770 km of footpaths, of many origins - drove roads, packhorse and miners' routes and turbary tracks. Britain's first long distance footpath, the Pennine Way, traverses the park for 51 km. The Park Committee have provided signposts, stiles and bridges and have a programme for repair and restoration. They are particularly concerned with the Three Peaks Walk which has become exceptionally eroded; for example 150,000 people climb Ingleborough each year. Active steps are being taken to restore a good surface across the very fragile upland soils. There is a large interpretive programme which is closely integrated with the general management of the park.

The Committee, through development control and conservation schemes, endeavours to maintain the rich heritage of unspoilt villages and to conserve landscape features such as isolated barns and other farm buildings, stone walls and traditional meadows. It provides a free advisory service, backed up with grants, to farmers and landowners for conservation work and on recreation facilities. There is an active management progamme on broadleaved woodlands and advice is provided on planting and management.

British Rail has resumed service during the spring and summer on the spectacular Settle to Carlisle railway, supplementing the Dales rail charter service. Residents and visitors can now once again reach areas that had become inaccessible.

Management plans:
National Park Plan Review 1984.

Land ownership:
Nearly all the land is in private ownership, only 2 per cent being publicly owned, divided between the National Trust (1.3 per cent), the National Park Committee, Yorkshire Water, the Nature Conservancy Council and the Ministry of Defence.

Natural areas of special interest:
National Nature Reserves: 2
Other nature reserves: 5 Yorkshire Wildlife Trust; 1 National Park Committee
Sites of Special Scientific Interest: 56 including Malham Tarn. Many of the caves are included in larger geomorphological SSSIs; 4 (Kinsey, Douky Bottom, Jubilee and Victoria) are also classified as ancient monuments.

The built environment:
Conservation areas: 18
Listed buildings: Being reviewed; 700 at mid-review; total likely to be over 1,200.

Historical sites and landscapes:
Archaeological sites: more than 60 stone circles, settlements, and burials; 3 Roman sites; 2 linear earthworks and 2 inscribed crosses
Others: 4 ecclesiastical buildings, 2 towers and 1 castle.

Administering authority:
Yorkshire Dales National Park Committee (North Yorkshire County Council),
Yorebridge House,
Bainbridge,
via Leyburn,
N. Yorks DL8 3BP
Tel: (0969) 50456

The Broads

Designated 1978   287 sq km

Desciption

The Norfolk and Suffolk Broads are the largest area of fresh water wetland in England, unique in landscape, history and appeal - "an enchanted land of mysterious misty fens, slow winding waterways, wet tangled woodlands and acres of marshes where cattle graze below an immense open sky." They lie in the lowlands of East Anglia in an area roughly bounded by the towns of Great Yarmouth, Lowestoft, Bungay, Norwich and North Walsham. Two rivers, the Bure and the Yare, flow into the sea at Great Yarmouth and it is the alluvial plains of these two rivers and their tributaries that form the area known as Broadland which, after many vicissitudes, came under the jurisdiction of the Broads Authority in 1978. Under the Norfolk and Suffolk Broads Bill, now before Parliament, the long term care of the Broads will be assured.

The River Bure, and its tributaries the Thurne and the Ant, drain the area north west of Yarmouth; the Yare flows broadly eastward from Norwich to the sea, while its tributary the Waveney flows east from Bungay to near Lowestoft where it turns sharply to the north, joining the Yare not far from its mouth.

Cockshot Dyke with mature, natural vegetation and clean, clear water. Man created the unique area of the Broads with his peat digging. In this century, lack of management, intensification of farming on the land and recreation on the water have seriously reduced the natural beauty and the scientific value but improvements are being made and will be furthered when the new Broads Authority is set up.

The character of the present Broads is largely a creation of man. There are navigable waterways, open broads, reed beds, fen, carr woodlands of willows and alder, reclaimed grazing marshlands and some cultivated lands. There are also 42 broads (areas of still, open water) covering about 800 ha within the flood plain of the rivers system that provides 200 km of navigable lock-free waterways. The Broads themselves are entirely manmade. Great beds of peat formed in the valleys of the East Anglian rivers after the end of the last Ice Age, over land that was affected by periodic invasion and recession of the sea. Large steep-sided peat cuttings were excavated in these beds for fuel in medieval times and these were flooded by a rise in sea level during the 13th century. The succession of vegetation which colonised these cuttings - plants of open water giving way to reed and sedge beds and finally to woodland - were in their turn exploited and managed. One product was the famous Norfolk reed used in thatching. Other areas were drained and turned into grazing marshes, rich in wetland plants and a paradise for wading birds; drainage mills are still an important feature of the landscape. The open waters were used for water transport - there are substantial docks in Norwich - and for fishing and wildfowling. Because the Broads area is strictly drawn the resident population is small, only 5,500. Villages are attractive, usually grouped round a riverside quay ("staithe") or village green.

The area has long been popular for recreation and a mecca for naturalists. About 250,000 take boating holidays each year and the total number of visitors using the water is probably 650-750,000. The decline in traditional economic uses has been paralleled by a massive growth in the use of the waterways for boating and by great pressure to intensify agricultural production from the grazing marshes. The delicately balanced plant and animal communities of the Broads have not been able to withstand these changes; but it is upon these communities that the character of the Broads ultimately depends.

Management

There has been a serious decline during the last 40 years in the natural beauty and scientific interest of the Broads; the problem has been to find effective solutions when so wide a range of interests and of local, regional and central government agencies are involved. Ever since a

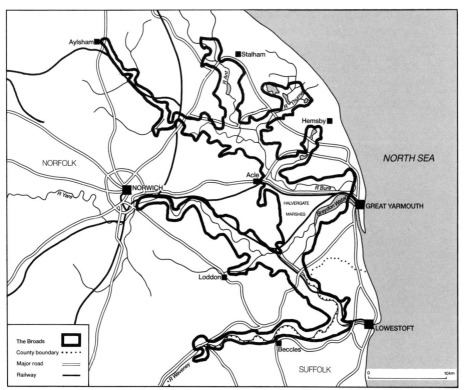

The Broads

proposal in the Hobhouse Report of 1947 to make the area into a national park was not accepted by the Government, there have been a number of initiatives to bring things under control. The Nature Conservancy's *Report on Broadland* in 1965 urged a strategic approach and stimulated the setting up of a Broadland Consortium which published a plan in 1971, but little was done. In 1976 the Countryside Commission reopened the question; and as a result a non-statutory Broads Authority was established in 1978. It arrested the decline and began to improve matters. The present Bill, the outcome of the most recent pressure for further action, proposes to set up a statutory Broads Authority which will have greater powers and more resources.

There are four sets of main problems:

- changes in water quality;
- bank erosion;
- the management of the fens;
- the management of the grazing marsh.

Water quality. The central problem has been the deterioration of the quality of the water which has resulted from increased levels of nitrates from farm run-off and phosphate from sewage effluent. These chemicals have stimulated the growth of microscopic algae at the expense of the larger water plants. A number of steps are being taken; the first and most important has been to reduce the levels of phosphate in sewage effluent and this is being carried out by the water authority, in conjunction with the Broads Authority, on selected rivers. In addition, the enriched mud has been pumped out from a number of broads and artificial plants are being tested as a means of encouraging the growth of tiny zooplankton, which will remove algae from the water.

Bank erosion. This is mainly caused by the growing number of motor boats aggravated by the loss of the vegetation of the banks. Measures are being taken to reduce the wash from the boats by introducing selective speed limits, the development of sympathetic hull designs and the restoration of vegetation by protecting the banks with netting and asphalt matting.

The Fens. The natural development of vegetation in open water leads to the build-up of peat and a gradual progression to dry land covered with bushes and trees (carr). In the past this process has been checked by cutting of reed, sedge and marsh hay, most of which has now ceased. An extensive programme of fen management work has been initiated to combat this neglect and is aimed at the many thousands of acres of fens in private ownership. Advice, grants and a crucial labour supply are provided, together with the specialist machinery needed. The same range of help is also available to a variety of conservation organisations who are already embarking on this vital work.

Grazing marsh. Over a quarter of the grazing marsh acreage has been lost to the plough to grow more wheat under incentives provided by the Common Agricultural Policy. The deepening and pollution of drains has led to a serious decline in wild plants; new barns, power cables and concrete roads have intruded on the landscape. The rate of arable conversion increased dramatically in the early 1980s; the Broads Authority found that Management Agreements were ineffective in stemming the tide and therefore they argued for an alternative approach. As a result an experiment, the Broads Grazing Marsh Conservation Scheme, to continue less intensive farming has been sponsored by the Countryside Commission and the Ministry of Agriculture, based on Halvergate Marshes and Haddiscoe Island. This voluntary scheme began in 1985, to run for three years; it offered a grant of £50/acre/year; 90 per cent of farmers opted for it. It has now been overtaken by the declaration of the Broads as an Environmentally Sensitive Area (see ESAs section); under this two levels of grant are offered - £50 for those who continue traditional methods and £80 for those willing to practise more positive management for wildlife.

Management plans:
>   Draft Strategy and Management Plan, 1982; Definitive version, 1987.
>   New authority must produce plan within three years of April, 1988. The new Environmentally Sensitive Area (ESA) includes the whole of the Broads Authority area.

Land ownership:
>   Mostly in private ownership; much owned by the local Naturalists' Trusts and the RSPB; National Trust 688 ha; Broads Authority 148 ha.

Natural areas of special interest:
>   National Nature Reserves: 2
>   Other nature reserves: 1 Local Nature Reserve.
>   Sites of Special Scientific Interest: 22
>   Areas of international importance: 2 sites under the Ramsar Convention in the Bure Marshes NNR.

The built environment:
>   Conservation areas: 11
>   Listed buildings: being reviewed; Horsey Windpump belongs to the National Trust.

Historic sites and landscapes:
>   Archaeological sites: none, but the peat diggings and research results from peat stratigraphy are of great archaeological importance.

Administering authority:
>   Broads Authority
>   Thomas Harvey House,
>   18 Colegate,
>   Norwich,
>   Norfolk NR3 1BQ
>   Tel: (0603) 610734

New Forest

Designated: 1079   375 sq km

Description

The New Forest lies between Southampton and Bournemouth in the south west of the county of Hampshire, bordering, for eight kilometres, the coastline of the Solent to the east of Lymington. It is one of those rare areas which are of unique merit - for its ecology, its history and its beauty. Nowhere else in lowland Britain is there still remaining a large expanse of uncultivated land on recent "soft" rocks. There are smaller areas elsewhere, but only in the New Forest can one lose oneself in a landscape of heath and bog, clear meandering streams and woods of venerable oak and beech, watch the deer and badger and imagine oneself in the Middle Ages. There is only one New Forest.

The Forest cannot be understood outside its historical context. The area has been a protected landscape for more than 900 years; during this time the purposes for which it has been preserved have changed several times, but in spite of this its integrity has been preserved. It was in about 1079 that William I created a royal hunting preserve to be called the "New" Forest. At that time the area was a wild area of woods, heaths and bogs with a scatter of farms and settlements. Although parts had certainly been cultivated since the Bronze Age, and there was a flourishing Roman pottery, the poor soils ensured that the population was small. The act of "afforestation" meant that no land could be enclosed with fences, which might prevent free movement of deer, but the people were allowed to continue grazing their stock.

The gentle contours of the New Forest are covered by a mixture of woodland, plantation and open space – heath, grassland, bracken and bog. The Commoners' grazing animals keep much of it open but active management is also needed to retain the 'lawns' and the much favoured edge, where the trees meet the grass.

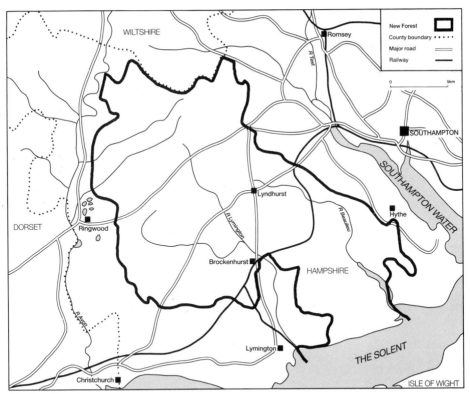

The New Forest

Few tree seedlings could survive the browsing of such numbers of animals and the woodlands began to retreat. So, beginning in the 15th century, there started a trend to enclose areas of the forest for the growing of timber, which was the most important raw material of the period. In 1698 the Crown assumed that the power of enclosure, by which up to 6,000 acres could be enclosed at any time and the animals of the commoners excluded, could be rolled on, as mature woods were thrown open, to allow further enclosure. This diminution of grazing was exacerbated by the competition from the deer, themselves grazing animals.

A critical situation developed by the mid-19th century. The sovereign no longer hunted deer (the last record was some 200 years earlier) and the way was open for a fundamental change in the management of the Forest. In 1851 the Deer Removal Act was passed, under which the deer were to be eliminated in return for the commoners' agreement that 10,000 acres of open land could be fenced and used for timber production; and all Rights of Common (to grazing, firewood, turf, marl and mast) were registered, the Court of Verderers being set up by statute to safeguard these.

This led to tension between the commoners and the Crown over enclosures, especially as it proved impossible to exterminate the deer; eventually, after examination by a Select Committee, the Crown gave up its rolling power of enclosure under the New Forest Act 1877. The beauty of the New Forest was used as an argument in evidence to this Committee and the scene was set for the present objectives of management - a balance between commoners' rights, the production of wood, the natural beauty of the Forest and its enjoyment by the public.

No other area in Britain has the combination of a large proportion of Crown land (now managed by the Forestry Commission) subject to common rights which are administered by a body set up by statute (the Verderers). It is to this balance of interest that the New Forest owes its survival into an age where the quality of landscape is nationally recognised.

The New Forest lies in the Hampshire Basin, a shallow depression in the chalk, which is filled with tertiary deposits of sands and clays laid down in shallow seas and by rivers. These were topped by later gravels and have since been eroded into a gentle landscape of gravel plateaux and shallow valleys. Poor sands and gravels covered with heath are more common in the north; richer loams and clays, well wooded, predominate in the south. There are extensive bogs in the valleys fed by springs where porous soils lie on top of the clay.

The Forest was once wholly covered in trees but early cultivation and grazing turned much of this into heath. The open forest now is a mosaic of heath and bog; grassland, furze and bracken; and woodland (the "Ancient and Ornamental Woodlands") - a mosaic which is mainly the result of natural change in the vegetation under the influence of fluctuating numbers of grazing animals and of ancient enclosures. The enclosable forest is a mixture of conifers and of broadleaved woodlands, predominantly oak and beech. All of these are of great value and interest for their plants and animals; the extent of the area, its continuity with the past, its variety of habitat and the quantities of "edge" all contribute to this richness. The Forest is one of the strongholds of the smooth snake and sand lizard, of the Dartford warbler and of many rare plants, among them the wild gladiolus.

The beauty of the Forest found its way into literature, in the late 18th century - William Gilpin, the exponent of the "picturesque", was the Vicar of Boldre in the New Forest. The changing combinations of heather and woodland, water and majestic trees, open vista and intimate retreat, the colour contrasts of heath, bracken, pine and oak, of the deep shade of forest and the brilliance of the open heath - all have a perennial appeal which brings ever increasing numbers to admire and enjoy.

Management

The management of the Crown land in the Forest (27,022 ha out of a total of 37,544 ha) is the responsibility of the Forestry Commission. It has been their difficult task to balance the production of timber, the rights of commoners, the claims of nature conservation, the beauty of the landscape, the trunk roads which pass through the Forest and the need to provide for the very large numbers who now visit the Forest. For example, the number of day visitors is estimated at 9.25 million a year and the number of camper/nights increased from 90,000 in 1956 to 800,000 in 1983.

The Commission is now guided in this by a policy statement given by the Minister of Agriculture in 1971 which gives specific, and for them unusual, directions.

There have been notable successes in reconciling the different interests:

- Since 1972 a firm policy has been implemented on access and recreation. Cars are excluded from the open forest and "wild camping" has been outlawed. Controlled car parking, camping and caravan sites have been provided (242 ha of car parks and camp sites).

- There is a Minute of Intent between the Forestry Commission and the Nature Conservancy Council recognising the whole Forest as of National Nature Reserve status, with close consultation on the management of the forest - especially on the Forestry Commissions's statutory obligation to drain and clear coarse herbage in the interest of the commoners' animals and on the management of the Ancient and Ornamental Woodlands.

- Deer numbers are limited to Red (70), Fallow (600), Roe (300) and Sika (60).

- The main through roads have been fenced to keep animals off them.

- The forest estate is managed, in spite of constraints, to produce 34,000 cu m of softwood and 4,000 cu m hardwood annually.

Management plans:
Management Plan 1972-1981; Management Plan 1982-1991. These have been agreed with the Verderers and the Nature Conservancy Council and are based on a policy statement (the Mandate) in 1971 and reaffirmed in 1982. The New Forest District Council has developed the New Forest Heritage Area.

Land ownership:
The largest part is Open Forest (Crown Land) (49 per cent); private commons, agricultural and residential land account for 28 per cent; the total inclosable land is 23 per cent of which Inclosures under the 1877 Act amount to 19 per cent and the remaining 4 per cent are Inclosures under the 1949/64 Acts, Crown freehold Inclosures and leasehold land.

Natural areas of special interest:
The whole New Forest is recognised to be of National Nature Reserve status and is scheduled as an SSSI. Its valley bogs, oceanic heaths and ancient forests are of international importance. It contains half the remaining area of Anglo-Norman heathland, the most important tract of this habitat in Europe.

The built environment:
Conservation areas: 13
Listed buildings: Being revised; over 800 in the parishes of the New Forest District (some of these are outside the boundaries of the "perambulation" of the New Forest).
Outstanding large houses and parks; Beaulieu Abbey, Rhinefield House, Moyles Court.

Historic sites and landscapes:
Archaeological sites: 96 including numerous barrows, earthworks and 4 Roman potteries.
Other: The whole New Forest is historic, the intact survival of a medieval hunting forest containing very numerous signs of past occupation, many as yet unidentified and unstudied.

Administering authority:
The Forestry Commission,
Office of the Deputy Surveyor of the New Forest,
The Queen's House,
Lyndhurst,
Hampshire SO4 7NH
Tel: (042 128) 3141

NATIONAL SCENIC AREAS

(Scotland)

The reasons why Scotland has no national parks are complex and have been partly explained in the Introduction. Yet one of Scotland's greatest assets and one that gives it international repute is its magnificent scenery of mountains and loch, wide heather covered moors and woodlands of pine and birch with the superb and shifting colours of its oceanic climate. The protection of this scenic heritage, and the need to enable people to enjoy it fully, have been a live issue for many years. To do so is an important part of the work of the Countryside Commission for Scotland.

After the publication in 1978 of a report by the Countryside Commission for Scotland on "Scotland's Scenic Heritage", the Secretary of State for Scotland made an Order under the 1972 Town and Country Planning (Scotland) Act designating 40 national scenic areas identified by the Commission in its report. This selection of sites, mainly in the north and west of the mainland and in the Islands, amount to 12.9 per cent of the land and inland-water surface of Scotland.

As a very high proportion of the land in the national scenic areas is privately owned, protection is mainly exercised through special development control procedures. In addition to the normal control of development under the Town and Country Planning Acts, the local authority is bound to consult the Countryside Commission for Scotland where the proposed change or development falls within certain categories:

Snow covered Schiehallion seen across the waters of Loch Rannoch is in one of the 40 National Scenic Areas of Scotland: areas of great variety and size but all of exceptional beauty. Many include SSSIs such as the woodlands of Caledonian pine – the Blackwood of Rannoch – seen on the lower hills across the loch.

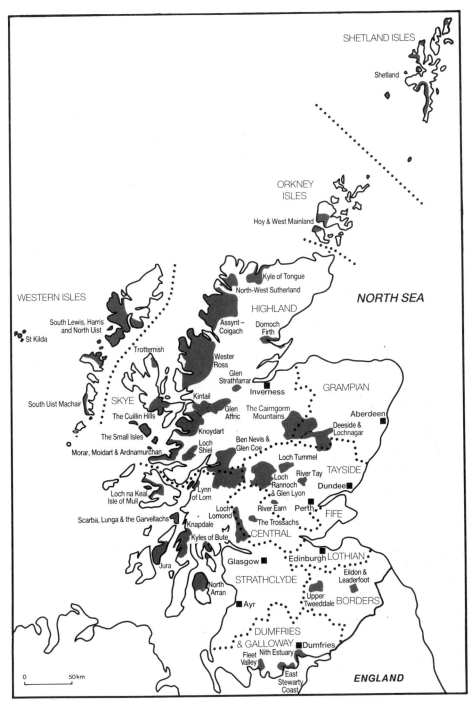

National Scenic Areas in Scotland

If the local authority wishes to proceed in a manner contrary to the policy and advice of the Countryside Commission for Scotland, the case must go before the Secretary of State for decision.

In addition to this statutory base, much has been done and continues to be done with goodwill and increased sensitivity to the natural beauty on the part of landowners and authorities.

The Town and Country Planning Acts, however, have little or no control over changes and developments in agriculture and forestry. To many it appears that the most potent threat to the highland landscape comes from new forestry plantations. Although consultation between the Forestry Commission, the local authorities and the Countryside Commission for Scotland take place where large-scale afforestation is proposed, no statutory control for the protection of landscape is, as yet, available, although the Countryside Comission for Scotland has made firm proposals in its policy publication, *Forestry in Scotland*. Legal provisions are available for making management agreements for the conservation of areas of high landscape value, but these have not yet been used.

In many ways stronger powers for conservation lie with other bodies. For example, at least thirteen of the national scenic areas contain areas owned or managed by the National Trust for Scotland, the main arm of the voluntary sector concerned with landscape protection. Ownership, in the hands of such a body as the National Trust for Scotland, confers the greatest protection. National scenic areas, therefore, which contain National Trust properties, are likely to be well protected. Benefactors, giving property to the Trust, have foreseen future changes and many have entered into conservation agreements which are a type of restrictive covenant for that particular property. Of the national scenic areas St Kilda belongs to the Trust and there are substantial holdings in Shetland (Fair Isle), Tongue, Wester Ross, Kintail, Ben Nevis and Glencoe, Loch Rannoch and Glen Lyon (Ben Lawers) and smaller holdings in others.

Change and development takes place on Trust property, but each proposal is considered on its merits, always against the background of the conservation of the natural beauty and heritage.

National scenic areas have a further degree of statutory protection where they coincide with national nature reserves and SSSIs. These are declared and notified by the Nature Conservancy Council. In national nature reserves the Nature Conservancy Council owns or manages the land for the well-being of wildlife and natural features. In the case of SSSIs the land managers are notified of activities detrimental to the value of the scientific value of the designated site and management agreements, possibly with compensation for potential loss of income, are entered into. Although these provisions do not have landscape protection as their prime objective, they do incidentally preserve landscape quality most effectively.

Shetland

Shetland Islands	15,600 ha	11 SSSIs (1 NNR)

Four areas of coast and two offshore islands having magnificent coastal scenery of cliffs, stacks, skerries, geos and caves. Includes the most northern point in the British Isles. Important colonies of nesting sea birds.

Hoy and West Mainland

Orkney Islands	14,800 ha	4 SSSIs

The spectacular sandstone cliffs and the rolling glaciated hills of Hoy (481 m) contrast with the cultivated lowlands of the west mainland. Many remains of ancient occupation.

Kyle of Tongue

Highland Region	18,500 ha	6 SSSIs (1 NNR)

The deeply indented sea loch of the Kyle of Tongue bordered with crofting settlements contrasts dramatically with Ben Hope (927 m) and Ben Loyal (764 m) rising from the moorland to the south.

North west Sutherland

Highland Region	20,500 ha	7 SSSIs (1 NNR)

Indented, rolling coastline and inland moorland of Lewisian gneiss from which rise the quartzite peaks of Ben Stack, Arkle and Foinaven (909 m). The island of Handa with bird colonies on sandstone cliffs.

Assynt-Coigach

Highland Region	90,200 ha	9 SSSIs (2 NNRs)

Dramatic landscape of rugged and strange-shaped hills of sandstone and quartzite rising from rolling glaciated terrain of peat bogs and lochans; Suilven and Stac Pollaidh are the most striking. An island of limestone round Inchnadamph provides a green contrast to the surrounding gneiss. Strongly indented coastline.

Wester Ross

Highland Region	145,300 ha	15 SSSIs (2 NNRs)

The most magnificent mountain landscape in the north of Scotland. Six great mountain groups of sandstone and quartzite strongly sculptured by glaciation and separated by coastal fjords and inland lochs. Caledonian pine forest and oak woods contrast with extensive moorland.

The sands of Gruinard Bay contrast with the rugged mountain scenery and the deep coastal fjords in the Wester Ross National Scenic Area. Some of the most magnificent scenery and the finest areas for wild life – there are 15 SSSIs – are found in this part of western Scotland.

Trotternish (Isle of Skye)

Highland Region   5,000 ha   3 SSSIs

Spectacular scenery of columnar basalt cliffs and pinnacles offset by green meadows and lochans produced by massive landslips. Below lie crofting settlements and moorland.

Cuillin Hills (Isle of Skye)

Highland Region   21,900 ha   2 SSSIs

The jagged gabbro of the Black Cuillin and the smooth pink granite of the Red Cuillin contrast to form a mountain area of great scenic splendour, penetrated by the narrow fjord of Loch Coruisk.

The Small Isles

Highland Region   15,500 ha   4 SSSIs (1 NNR)

The islands of Rhum, Eigg, Muck and Canna provide a perfect foil to one another and their characteristic shapes enrich the view from many places on the west coast - the mountainous Rhum, low-lying Canna and Muck and Eigg with its battleship shape dominated by the lava Sgurr.

Morar, Moidart and Ardnamurchan

Highland Region   15,900 ha   7 SSSIs

A gentle coastal landscape of great diversity and interest with the Small Isles in the background. Rocky and sandy bays with wooded slopes.

Loch Sheil

Highland Region   13,400 ha   5 SSSIs

A deep narrow fjord winding between the spurs of precipitous mountains.
Glenfinnan has strong historical associations with the Jacobite uprising.

Knoydart

Highland Region   39,500 ha   9 SSSIs

Strongly glaciated and rugged mountain country penetrated by the two magnificent sea lochs of Loch Nevis and Loch Hourn. One of the most remote and inaccessible parts of the Highlands and one of the wildest and most beautiful.

Kintail

Highland Region   16,300 ha   2 SSSIs

In a few miles the River Shiel plunges from the main east-west watershed of Scotland into Loch Duich, bordered on both north and south by steep, smooth contoured grass covered mountains with sharp ridges and sculptured corries.

Glen Affric

Highland Region   19,300 ha   2 SSSIs

The Glen contains one of most extensive remnants of the native Caledonian pine forest along the slopes above Loch Beinn a'Mheadhoin and Loch Affric. The high mountain ridge to the north is framed by water and majestic trees.

Glen Strathfarrar

Highland Region   3,800 ha   1 SSSIs (1 NNR)

Steep sided glen with extensive natural pine forest and backdrop of high mountains beyond Loch Beannacharan.

Dornoch Firth

Highland Region   7,500 ha   3 SSSIs

A shallow winding firth with bays, sands, flats, shallows and promontories, bordered at the seaward end by pasture and arable farm land rising, inland, to rounded granitic hills, wooded on the lower slopes.

Ben Nevis and Glen Coe

Highland/Tayside/Strathclyde   101,600 ha   16 SSSIs (1NNR)

Three valleys (Glen Etive, Glen Coe and Glen Nevis) ascend steeply from their sea lochs through dramatic country of high mountains, Ben Nevis (1141 m) being the highest in Britain. The rivers all rise on the wild and desolate Moor of Rannoch - once the focus of glaciation in this part of Scotland.

The Cairngorm Mountains

Highland Region/Grampian   67,200 ha   6 SSSIs (1NNR)

The high plateau of the Cairngorms is the most extensive area over 1000 m in Britain with four summits (Cairngorm, Ben Macdhui, Cairn Toul and Braeriach) over 1200 m; its scale is unmatched elsewhere. Seen from below the rounded slopes and sculptured corries are framed by remnants of the Caledonian pine forest.

South Lewis, Harris and North Uist

Western Isles   108,600 ha   12 SSSIs

Exposed mountain and moorland of the Outer Islands with crofting landscape, machair, wide sandy beaches and rocky headlands.

St Kilda

Western Isles   900 ha   NNR

Dramatic volcanic islands and isolated stacks with sheer cliffs (370 m) teeming with nesting gannets and other seabirds. The gentle slopes of the Village Bay with its deserted township add poignancy to the scene. Now a World Heritage Site.

South Uist Machair

Western Isles   6,100 ha   4 SSSIs (1NNR)

Wide soft landscape of sea, flower-rich machair, beaches of snowy shell sand and shallow lochans.

Deeside and Lochnagar

Grampian Region/Tayside   40,000 ha   9 SSSIs (2 NNRs)

The broad valley of the Dee with the pine forest of Ballochbuie and the parkland of Balmoral backed by the high plateau and corries of Lochnagar.

Loch Tummel

Tayside   9,200 ha   5 SSSIs

An intimate blend of loch, heather hills, birch and oak woods with small farms and mature plantations of conifers. Famed for the Queen's View.

Loch Rannoch and Glenlyon

Tayside/Central Region   48,400 ha   9 SSSIs (2 NNRs)

The open landscape of Loch Rannoch with its pine and birch woods backed by the graceful cone of Schiehallion contrasts with the rich, grass-covered hills of the narrow winding Glenlyon. Ben Lawers is famous for its arctic-alpine plants.

River Tay (Dunkeld)

Tayside   5,600 ha   7 SSSIs

The broad strath of the Tay lies between the low hills on the line of the Highland Border Fault - a harmonious pattern of rich farmland, birch and oakwood, plantations of conifers, especially larch, and Dunkeld with its cathedral and "Little Houses" of the 17th century.

River Earn (Comrie and St Fillans)

Tayside   3,000 ha   1 SSSIs

Where lowland meets highland - a mosaic of farmland and rocky pasture in a setting of heather-covered hills.

Loch na Keal, Isle of Mull

Strathclyde   12,700 ha   7 SSSIs

A varied seascape studded with small islands, including Staffa with the famous columnar basalt of Fingal's Cave; sea lochs bordered with wood, pasture and moorland.

Lynn of Lorn

Strathclyde   4,800 ha   3 SSSIs

Arms of the sea run betwen low, parallel ridges of limestone with rich farmland, luxuriant oakwoods and the parkland of large houses.

Scarba, Lunga and the Garvellachs

Strathclyde   1,900 ha   1 SSSIs

A varied group of islands of contrasting rocks and shapes - the Garvellachs, on which are the oldest ecclesiastical buildings in Scotland, set in an sea with fierce tide races.

Jura

Strathclyde   21,800 ha   2 SSSIs

The shapely quartzite cones of the Paps of Jura (7-800 m) rising from rolling moorland dominate the views from the coast of mid-Argyll.

Knapdale

Strathclyde   19,800 ha   6 SSSIs

Long parallel rock ridges penetrated by narrow arms of the sea and by freshwater lochs form the setting for a varied landscape of woodland, plantation, moor and farmland.

Kyles of Bute

Strathclyde   4,400 ha   2 SSSIs

Enclosed arms of the sea between steep, rocky, well wooded hill slopes with the moorland of the island of Bute to the south.

North Arran

Strathclyde   23,800 ha   5 SSSIs (1 NNR)

The rugged granite peaks (Goat Fell, 874 m) and deep glens rise from cultivated raised beaches and the rich vegetation of the coast. A highland outlier in the gentle landscape bordering the Firth of Clyde.

Loch Lomond

Strathclyde/Central   27,400 ha   12 SSSIs (1 NNR)

The Loch lies across the Highland Boundary Fault. The north is narrow, fjord-like; the south, with its richly wooded islands, lies in more open landscape backed by the coniferous plantations of the Queen Elizabeth Forest Park and by shapely Ben Lomond (974 m).

The Trossachs

Central   4,600 ha   1 SSSIs

On a smaller scale than the Highlands, a magnificent blend of woodland, loch and mountain. A celebrated literary beauty spot associated with Scott and Ruskin.

Upper Tweeddale

Borders   12,300 ha   2 SSSIs

A winding valley of farmland, pasture and varied woods with buildings of many periods, widening at intervals to give extensive views to the higher rounded grassy hills beyond.

Eildon and Leaderfoot

Borders   3,600 ha   6 SSSIs

A humane and cultivated landscape round Melrose in the wide fertile valley of the Tweed with abbeys and mansion houses, backed by the volcanic Eildon hills, beloved of Walter Scott.

Nith Estuary

Dumfries and Galloway   9,300 ha   6 SSSIs (2 NNRs)

An extensive horizontal landscape of sands, mudflats and saltings where the River Nith and Lochar Water flow into the Solway Firth, framed in cultivated and wooded lowlands.

East Stewartry Coast

Dumfries and Galloway   5,200 ha   2 SSSIs

A contrast between tidal flats and surrounding moorland hills with well wooded lower slopes and promontories. Traditional villages.

Fleet Valley

Dumfries and Galloway   5,300 ha   3 SSSIs

The village of Gatehouse of Fleet marks the change from the estuary to an inner valley with rich farmland, flanking woodlands and moorland above.

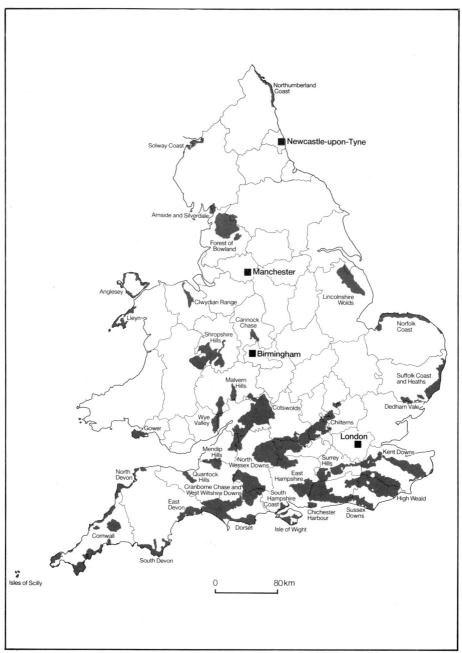

Northumberland
Coast

■ Newcastle-upon-Tyne

Solway Coast

Arnside and Silverdale

Forest of
Bowland

■ Manchester

Anglesey

Lincolnshire
Wolds

Clwydian Range

Cannock
Chase

Lleyn

Norfolk
Coast

Shropshire
Hills

■ Birmingham

Suffolk Coast
and Heaths

Malvern
Hills

Wye
Valley

Cotswolds

Dedham Vale

Chilterns

Gower

London

Kent Downs

Mendip
Hills

Surrey
Hills

North
Wessex Downs

North
Devon

Quantock
Hills

East
Hampshire

Cranborne Chase and
West Wiltshire Downs

East
Devon

South
Hampshire
Coast

High Weald

Chichester
Harbour

Sussex
Downs

Cornwall

Dorset

Isle of Wight

South Devon

Isles of Scilly

0   80 km

Areas of Outstanding Natural Beauty in England and Wales

OTHER PROTECTED LANDSCAPES

Areas of Outstanding Natural Beauty (England and Wales)

Areas of outstanding natural beauty (generally known as AONBs) are parts of the countryside of England and Wales which lack the extensive areas of open country which would make them suitable for the status of national park but are, nevertheless, of such high landscape quality that there is a national interest in keeping them so.

These areas are designated by the Secretary of State for the Environment or the Secretary of State for Wales under Section 87 of the National Parks and Access to the Countryside Act 1949, on the recommendation of the Countryside Commisssion. There are now 37 AONBs, amounting to 17,084 sq km or 11.3 per cent of the total area of England and Wales. Proposals for the designation of the North Pennines and Howardian Hills AONBs are being considered by the Secretary of State; four additional areas are also proposed. Boundaries of some existing AONBs are now being reviewed.

Present policies are based on a statement by the Secretary of State for the Environment on 29 July 1982 following a reappraisal of the value of AONBs by the Countryside Commission in 1980. The principal objective is the conservation of natural beauty, but full regard must be paid to the economic and social well-being of the areas. The provision of recreation is not a formal objective; it should be met, but only in so far as this is consistent with the conservation of natural beauty and the needs of agriculture, forestry and other users. Neither is nature conservation a formal objective, except in so far as it is included in the statutory definition of "natural beauty". But the AONBs do contain a large proportion of land which is designated SSSI or is managed as a nature reserve*, and the conditions affecting changes in land use in these provide an additional safeguard.

* For example in Wales: Anglesey AONB - 28 sites (1 NNR) 22.6 per cent; Clwydian AONB - 6 sites 1 per cent; Gower AONB - 16 sites (3 NNR) 31.5 per cent; Lleyn AONB - 9 sites (2 NNR) 7.9 per cent; Wye - 17 sites (1 NNR) 1.5 per cent.

The village of Belchford lies on the lower chalk near the south-western edge of the Lincolnshire Wolds AONB. Behind is higher ground of chalk with a view point looking over the lowlands of the county. It is an area of intensive agriculture, only the steeper scarps and a few sinuous valleys remaining unplanted but none the less a fine area of agricultural landscapes.

The most significant effect of designation as AONB is to lift on to the national plane the level of awareness about the area, its quality and its problems; there will be a national interest in the conservation and enhancement of its natural beauty and greater national resources can be made available for it. Designation should not be a serious impediment to most forms of development, but it is an indication that great care should be taken over even the smallest developments so that these are carried out in such a way that they do not disturb the quality of the landscape and its legacy of buildings.

The benefits accorded by AONB status are:-

- it makes it less likely that the government or public agencies will propose major new intensive developments such as reservoirs, roads or power stations;

- it strengthens the hand of the planning authority in rejecting proposals for new urban development which would be out of character and in obtaining high standards of design;

- it makes it more likely that funds will be found (from local authorities and the Countryside Commission) for conservation measures, including management agreements and tree planting;

- it encourages the appointment of ranger services which help farmers to solve problems caused by the number of visitors;

- it increases the chances that owners may gain fiscal relief from capital transfer tax.

The local limestone buildings of Lower Slaughter in the Cotswolds AONB are typical of the beautiful villages of this area. Many of these villages lie in deep wooded valleys – often along clear streams – while the windswept hills are now covered with arable crops. These have displaced the sheep of historical times which provided the wealth for fine wool churches in the small market towns.

Although local authorities are not **required** to set up any special machinery to plan and manage AONBs they are encouraged to nominate an officer to have general oversight and responsibility for coordinating strategic and management plans. They are also encouraged to prepare a Statement of Intent and management plans for areas where there is conflict over land use as well as action to resolve it if feasible. Where an AONB falls under the jurisdiction of more than one local authority, they are encouraged to form a Joint Advisory Committee.

Areas of Outstanding Natural Beauty
England and Wales

	Date of designation order	Date of confirmation order	Area in sq km
Gower	May 1956	Dec 1956	189
Quantock Hills	May 1956	Jan 1957	99
Lleyn	Sep 1956	May 1957	155
Northumberland Coast	Sep 1956	Mar 1958	129
Surrey Hills	Sep 1956	May 1958	414
Cannock Chase	Jun 1958	Sep 1958	68
Shropshire Hills	Jul 1958	Mar 1959	777
Dorset	Dec 1957	Jul 1959	1036
Malvern Hills	Mar 1959	Oct 1959	104
Cornwall	Apr 1959	Oct 1959	932
Extension	Mar 1981	Oct 1983	25
North Devon	Sep 1959	May 1960	171
South Devon	Sep 1959	Aug 1960	332
East Hampshire	Jun 1961	Sep 1962	391
East Devon	Jan 1963	Sep 1963	267
Isle of Wight	Mar 1963	Sep 1963	189
Chichester Harbour	Jul 1963	Feb 1964	75
Forest of Bowland	Feb 1963	Feb 1964	803
Solway Coast	Sep 1964	Dec 1964	107
Chilterns	May 1964	Dec 1965	800
Sussex Downs	Jun 1965	Apr 1966	981
Cotswolds	Feb 1966	Aug 1966	1507
Anglesey	Dec 1966	Nov 1967	215
South Hampshire Coast	May 1967	Dec 1967	78
Norfolk Coast	May 1967	Apr 1968	450
Kent Downs	Dec 1967	Jul 1968	845
Suffolk Coasts and Heaths	Oct 1969	Mar 1970	391
Dedham Vale	Feb 1970	May 1970	57
Extension	Feb 1978	Aug 1978	15
Wye Valley	Feb 1971	Dec 1971	325
North Wessex Downs	Dec 1971	Dec 1972	1738
Mendip Hills	Feb 1972	Dec 1972	202
Arnside and Silverdale	Jul 1972	Dec 1972	75
Lincolnshire Wolds	Feb 1973	Apr 1973	560
Isles of Scilly	Oct 1975	Feb 1976	16
High Weald	Dec 1980	Oct 1983	1450
Cranborne Chase and West Wiltshire Downs	Dec 1981	Oct 1983	960
Clwydian Range	Jun 1984	Jul 1985	156

			17,084

16,252 square kilometres in England and 832 square kilometres in Wales; 11.3 per cent of the total area of England and Wales (151,096 square kilometres).

Awaiting designation: Howardian Hills, North Pennines;
Future proposals: Tamar and Tavy Valleys, Blackdown Hills, Berwyn Mountains and the Nidderdale Moors.

The Countryside Commission's policies for improving the control of development in AONBs are:

- Local authorities should adopt and apply development control policies which emphasise the conservation of natural beauty.

- New major industrial or commercial development should be regarded as inconsistent with the aims of designation, except when such developments are in the national interest and there is no alternative.

- Applications for substantial new mineral workings, or extensions to existing workings, should be subject to the most rigorous examination.

- Schemes for major roads and motorways should be examined with particular care to ensure that they are really necessary and that the route has been chosen to minimise damage.

- Extension or creation of small scale industries or commercial units in or near towns and villages should be in sympathy with the architecture and landscape of the area.

- Local authorities should establish informal notification arrangements with farmers in AONBs in cooperation with the National Farmers' Union, Farmers' Union of Wales and the Country Landowners' Association.

- Government departments and agencies** should improve their consultation on major developments to make them subject to greater public scrutiny.

** The Forestry Commission has agreed to consult with the Countryside Commission on all applications for grant aid towards new planting in AONBs. High priority for grant-aid, up to a maximum of 50 per cent, is given to all eligible proposals for grant, provided that these are consistent with the conservation of natural beauty; up to 75 per cent can be provided towards management agreements.

Areas of Outstanding Natural Beauty (Northern Ireland)

The Conservation Service of the Department of the Environment for Northern Ireland is the government body which has been given authority to protect the best natural, unspoilt and scenic areas of Northern Ireland. Its aim is to maintain and enhance the quality of the countryside and to provide enjoyment and pleasure for present and future generations. It also has a responsibility to conserve plant and animal communities and a range of protected sites representative of natural conditions and features found in Northern Ireland (a responsibility carried in England, Wales and Scotland by the Nature Conservancy Council).

The area of outstanding natural beauty is, at present, the only category of protected landscape which is used in Northern Ireland. Although there is power to designate national parks under both the 1965 Act and 1985 Order, the Department of the Environment considers that, in the present Northern Ireland context, it is better to conserve landscape and natural beauty through the development and management of AONBs. It does not therefore, for the foreseeable future, intend to designate any national parks.

AONBs are designated under Article 14 of the Nature Conservation and Amenity Lands (Northern Ireland) Order 1985. Under this legislation the Department may formulate proposals in relation to any AONB for:-

1. conserving or enhancing the natural beauty or amenities of the area;

2. conserving wildlife, historic objects or natural phenomena within it;

The Mourne AONB in Northern Ireland was designated in December 1986. The magnificent mountains are the core of the area. They are surrounded by foothills where farming is the main land use. In order to maintain the traditional character of the landscape, the periphery has been declared an environmentally sensitive area.

3.   promoting its enjoyment by the public;

4.   providing and maintaining public access to it.

The Department is advised by the Ulster Countryside Committee and by the Committee for Nature Conservation on matters to do with the countryside and nature conservation.

The Conservation Service coordinates policies and management for the AONBs through liaison with other parts of central or local government. Town and Country Planning powers are administered by the Planning Service of the Department of the Environment for Northern Ireland; agricultural, forestry and drainage powers by the Department of Agriculture for Northern Ireland; and recreation and access by the local authorities. Some AONBs fall within the area of a number of local authorities.

Following the new legislation - Nature Conservation and Amenity Lands Order (Northern Ireland) 1985 - the areas of AONB designation under the old Amenity Lands Act 1965 are being reviewed. This is based upon a change in emphasis away from development control to a broader conservation objective achieved through evolving and implementing policies relating to the protection of the prized countryside contained in the AONB. Land use, of which agriculture is a key part, is given its due importance along with planning and consideration of scenery. Nature conservation and heritage features are all part of this integrated appraisal of the countryside.

This preamble is necessary because only one AONB, Mourne, designated in 1986 and of just over 57,000 ha, can be accurately cited. The remaining areas are all based upon the unrevised old AONBs.

Mourne. A central core of 12 peaks of 600-700 metres in height, fringed on the east by a coastal plain of a unique stone-walled settlement pattern. To the south lies Carlingford Lough - the only fjord feature on the east coast of Ireland; and to the north a group of low hills around Slieve Croob. This montane granite landscape is penetrated by a series of deep river valleys where the juxtaposition of man's activities with the open moorland gives a variety of scenery of farming, forestry and moorland which is highly valued.

Areas of Outstanding Natural Beauty in Northern Ireland

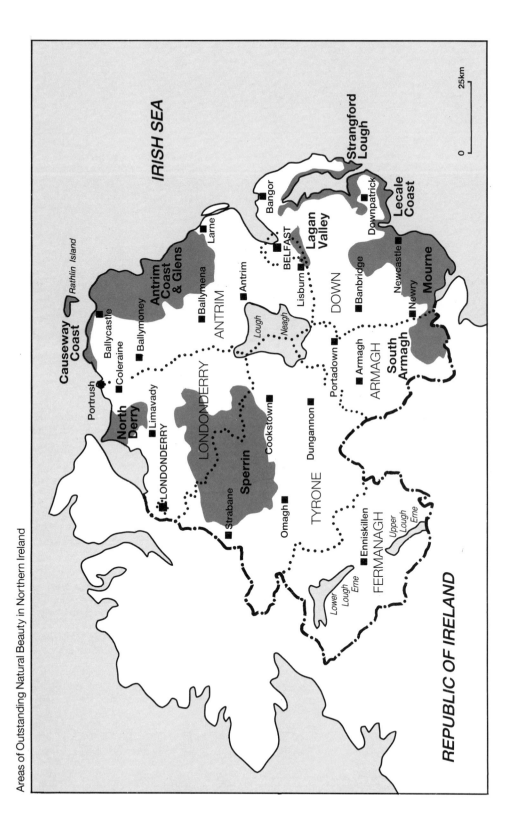

The **Antrim AONB** is being redesignated as the **Antrim Coast and Glens AONB** and the **Causeway Coast AONB**. The total area of both together is about 72,000 ha. The division reflects the variety and differences which will be manifest in the policies for each. The **Antrim Coast and Glens AONB** is characterised by a series of high headlands and intervening bays backed with steep-sided glens dissecting a high basalt plateau. These eastern running glens contrast with several wide and gentle valleys opening westwards with agricultural and archeological interests.

The **Causeway Coast AONB** is a mainly cliff-edged, north-facing coast interspersed with fine stretches of strand and, in places, dunes. Behind the cliff edge there is a high open landscape with little topographical shelter. The original clachan settlement pattern with associated strip farms can still be traced in places. The traditional fishing communities are centred on small, sheltered, rocky inlets for which the name harbour is a considerable overstatement. The clan system of medieval Ireland is reflected in the number of inaccessible ruined castles along the coast.

Other AONBs still to be reviewed are as follows:-

South Armagh (c 10,000 ha). A compact area centred on Slieve Gullion Mountain, the plug of an extinct volcano, surrounded by farmland, 2-4 km wide, which in turn is contained by the heath covered Ring of Gullion, formed by the side vents of the central plug.

Sperrin (>10,000 ha). An extensive area of high ground west of the Lough Neagh lowlands, heavily glaciated and with its main relief running east to west. Within it the Glenelly, the Owenkillew and the Owenreagh form very picturesque, steepsided river valleys where agricultural settlement and land use contrast with the shrubby sides of the valleys and the heather-covered moorland. Small remnants of mature oakwood and modern forestry give variety and diversity to the scenery.

North Derry (c 13,000 ha). The Sperrins end in the north with a zone of cliffs overlooking the North Atlantic and with the eight kilometre long Magilligan strand at the sea mouth of the Foyle estuary. The steep, round-topped grassland hills and the accreting sandy shoreline are dominant features, separated from the rocky shore of Donegal by just one kilometre of sea.

Strangford Lough (c 19,000 ha). This low-lying area in the drumlin belt of North Down has been flooded by the obstruction caused by the narrow entrance and exit to the Irish sea. The tips of the drumlins thus flooded form a myriad of islands, especially on the western edge, with the Lough irregularly running between. The sheltered, deep waters are a natural resort for yachting and boating.

Lecale Coast (c 3,000 ha). The coastal area between Strangford Lough and the Mourne is a low, sometimes sandy, rocky or grassy shoreline. Its southern tip lies along an extensive sand and dune system, much of which is used by the Ministry of Defence.

Lagan Valley (c 2,000 ha). The pleasant, pastoral agricultural land of the Lagan Vally, on either side of the River Lagan, lies in the green belt of the Belfast/Lisburn conurbation. Its designation as an AONB was primarily a response to pressure for development.

Heritage Coasts

One of the main recommendations springing from the study of coastal preservation and development, begun by the then National Parks Commission in 1966 and culminating in 1970 in the publication by the Countryside Commission of the two reports *The Coastal Heritage* and *The Planning of the Coastline*, was the proposal that selected stretches of undeveloped coastline should be given a special protective designation as "Heritage Coasts". The Government response to this recommendation was set out in a joint Department of the Environment/Welsh Office Circular *The Planning of the Undeveloped Coastline*, issued in 1972. This welcomed the concept and recommended local authorities to define heritage coasts in their development plans and to prepare management plans for them in consultation with the Commission, but it was decided not to adopt any new statutory designation.

Much has been achieved since 1972. Thirty nine separate heritage coasts, representing the finest coastal scenery, have been defined stretching along 1370 km of coast (over 31 per cent of the total coastline of England and Wales) and only four new proposed coasts await definition. The landward depth of heritage coasts averages 2-3 kilometres.

Most heritage coasts coincide with the coastal frontages of established national parks and AONBs; many correspond with SSSIs. Key stretches of heritage coasts, too, have been acquired by the National Trust as part of Operation Neptune.

The definition of an heritage coast entitles it to receive special attention in planning and funds can more readily be directed towards its management; an important feature of this is the reconciliation of the conservation of the coast with its use for recreation and tourism. Three pilot projects for the planning and management of heritage coasts were successfully completed in the late 1970s (Glamorgan, Suffolk and Purbeck). These showed conclusively the importance of a heritage coast officer in achieving effective coastal conservation and recreation management.

Brancaster Staithe on the North Norfolk Heritage Coast. Over 31 per cent of the total coastline of England and Wales has been defined as heritage coast. Definition brings special attention in planning, funding and improved management.

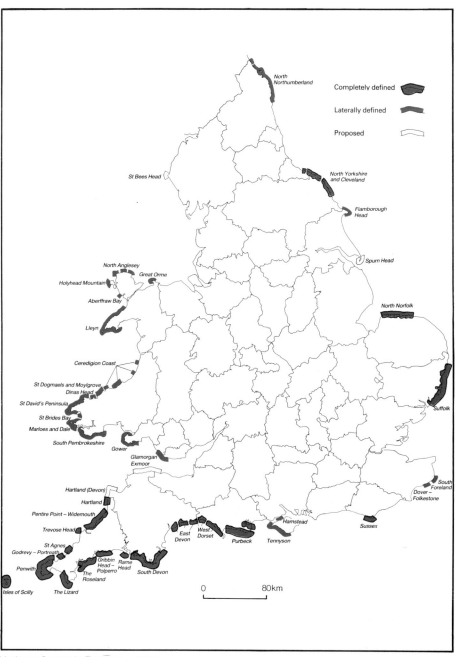

Heritage Coasts in England and Wales

Three-quarters of the defined heritage coasts now have staff including ranger services; and much the same number have prepared, or are preparing, Heritage Coast Management Plans.

In 1984 the Purbeck heritage coast was awarded the Council of Europe's Diploma for Conservation.

The total length of heritage coasts (on April 1, 1987) was 1370 km; this is 31.05 per cent of the coastline of England and Wales (4411.6 km).

Heritage Coasts (England and Wales)

(These are listed in clockwise order round the coast; capitals indicate those that are completely defined with inland areas; lower case letters indicate those that are laterally defined just as stretches along the coastline itself.)

	Date defined	Length in km
North Northumberland	Feb 73	92.7
NORTH YORKSHIRE & CLEVELAND	May 81	54.7
Flamborough Head	Oct 79	18.5
NORTH NORFOLK	Apr 75	63.2
SUFFOLK	Sep 79	56.3
South Foreland	Nov 75	6.9
Dover-Folkestone	Nov 75	7.2
SUSSEX	Apr 73	13.3
Hamstead	Jul 74	11.3
Tennyson	Jul 74	32.8
PURBECK - East Section	Jun 81	9.6
PURBECK - West Section	Jun 81	42.0
WEST DORSET	Feb 84	39.7
EAST DEVON	Jun 84	28.3
SOUTH DEVON	Dec 86	74.4
RAME HEAD	Jan 76	6.8
GRIBBIN HEAD-POLPERRO	Jan 76/Apr 86	24.0
THE ROSELAND	Jan 76/Apr 86	54.2
THE LIZARD	Jan 76/Apr 86	27.9
PENWITH	Jan 76/Apr 86	54.8
ISLES OF SCILLY	Dec 75	64.4
GODREVY-PORTREATH	Jan 76/Apr 86	10.2
ST AGNES	Jan 76/Apr 86	11.0
TREVOSE HEAD	Jan 76/Apr 86	3.5
PENTIRE POINT-WIDEMOUTH	Jan 76/Apr 86	54.1
HARTLAND (Cornwall)	Jan 76/Apr 86	10.9
Glamorgan	Jun 73	21.7
Gower	Jun 73	55.0
South Pembrokeshire	Jul 74	66.0
Marloes and Dale	Jul 74	43.3
St Brides Bay	Jul 74	8.0
St David's Peninsula	Jul 74	82.0
Dinas Head	Jul 74	17.7
St Dogmaels and Moylgrove	Jul 74	22.5
Ceredigion Coast	Dec 82	33.8
Lleyn	Mar 74	88.3
Aberffraw Bay	Jul 73	7.7
Holyhead Mountain	Jul 73	12.9
North Anglesey	Jul 73	28.6
Great Orme	Mar 74	7.1

An additional 80 km are proposed at Spurn Head, Exmoor, Hartland (Devon) and St Bees Head.

Environmentally Sensitive Areas

In recent years much of the harm done to the natural beauty of the countryside has been caused by changes in the practices and structure of agriculture and forestry; these effects could only be softened in national parks and, for nature conservation, in SSSIs. Until 1985 there seemed to be no possibility that the money available for national agricultural support could be used to encourage less intensive and more environmentally sensitive methods of farming.

A very significant start was made towards changing the situation with the promulgation on 12 March 1985 of Article 19 of Council Regulation (EEC) No. 797/85 on improving the efficiency of agricultural structures.

Halvergate Marshes in the Norfolk Broads were among the first group of environmentally sensitive areas. This status makes the farmers eligible for grant aid from MAFF to maintain the traditional land use of unimproved hay meadows and grazing marshes which are a haven for wildlife and an increasingly rare type of landscape.

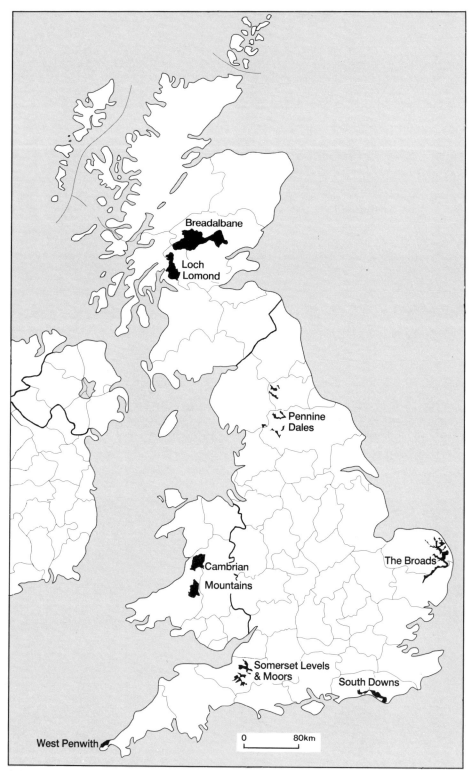

Breadalbane

Loch Lomond

Pennine Dales

Cambrian Mountains

The Broads

Somerset Levels & Moors

South Downs

West Penwith

0   80km

Environmentally Sensitive Areas

Article 19
Council Regulation (EEC) No. 797/85

1. In order to contribute towards the introduction or continued use of agricultural production practices compatible with the requirements of conserving the natural habitat and ensuring an adequate income for farmers, Member States are authorised to introduce special national schemes in environmentally sensitive areas.

2. For the purpose of this article, "environmentally sensitive areas" means in particular areas of recognised importance from an ecological and landscape point of view.

3. The aid may be granted to farmers who undertake to farm environmentally important areas so as to preserve or improve their environment.

   The farmer's undertaking must stipulate at least that there will no further intensification of agricultural production and that the stock density and the level of intensity of agricultural production will be compatible with the specific environmental needs of the area concerned.

4. Member States shall forward to the Commission all such prospective schemes, together with a list of areas qualifying for aid under those schemes.

From lists of possible candidate sites prepared by the Countryside Commissions, the Nature Conservancy Council, English Heritage, Cadw and the Department of the Environment for Northern Ireland, 14 proposals for England and Wales were submitted to the Government, two for Scotland and one for Northern Ireland. As a first stage, six environmentally sensitive areas (ESAs), all in England and Wales, were designated in August 1986 by the Minister of Agriculture. All but one of these lie outside national parks but often coincide with areas which are of high scientific interest. They cover about 1800 sq km (just over one per cent of England and Wales). Two ESAs in Scotland, Loch Lomond and Breadalbane, have now been designated and consideration is being given to the Mourne Mountains in Northern Ireland.

The detailed criteria set by the Ministry of Agriculture Fisheries and Food (MAFF) and the Department of Agriculture and Fisheries for Scotland (DAFS) were that the ESAs should be areas:

1.   of national environmental significance;

2.   whose conservation depends on the adoption, maintenance or extension of a particular form of farming practice;

3.   in which there have occurred, or there is a likelihood of, changes in farming practices which pose a major threat to the environment;

4.   which represent a discrete and coherent unit of environmental interest;

5.   which would permit the economical administration of appropriate conservation aids.

Under this imaginative scheme farmers in the ESAs will be encouraged to volunteer to adopt or continue farming practices which will safeguard the characteristic landscape, wildlife and archaeological features of each area. In return they will receive compensation payments of from £30 to £200/ha/year; these will apply to features such as grazing land, hedges, broadleaved woodlands, archaeological features, barns and stone walls. The agreements will be binding for five years in the first instance. First indications are that the majority of farmers will choose to enter the scheme.

The Government has announced its intention to designate a further six ESAs in England and Wales - North Peak, Breckland, Suffolk River Valleys, Test Valley, Shropshire Borders (Clun) and Lleyn - and to extend the existing ESAs in the Cambrian Mountains and the South Downs. These first 12 ESAs may provide a model for management in the wider countryside.

Broads

This area largely coincides with that under the jurisdiction of the Broads Authority (see "The Broads"). The new measures are effectively a continuation and expansion of the Broads Grazing Marshes Scheme instituted by the Countryside Commission.

Characteristics: open water, reed-beds, fen and fen woodland, meadows and grazing marshes. The open-water Broads are the result of medieval peat diggings. Rich in wildlife everywhere, especially in species of fen, open water and ditches, unimproved hay meadows and grazing marshes. Farming arable, livestock or mixed. *Threats from farming*: transforming grazing marshes to arable or re-seeded pasture; deepening or filling in of drainage dykes; reduced grazing stock and abandonment of grazings; lowered water tables and nitrogen run-off. *Objectives of management*: maintain the features of landscape, wildlife and archaeological interest by encouraging the continuance of traditional livestock farming where it still occurs and its expansion into some areas that are now managed more intensively.

Pennine Dales

Characteristics: the upper parts a number of Dales, including parts of the Yorkshire Dales National Park, each a landscape of hay meadows, wet meadows, pasture and rough grazing, small woods, dry stone walls and field barns. Rich flora and wading birds on the wet pastures. Fine archaeological landscapes. Farming under adverse conditions of hill sheep, store cattle and some dairying. *Threats from farming*: drainage, reseeding, fertilising, abandonment of hay making, neglect of barns, walls and woods, inappropriate new buildings. *Objectives of management*: maintain the small-scale landscape pattern and the richness in plants and animals of unimproved grasslands.

Somerset Levels

Characteristics: one of the two largest surviving areas of wetland in England. Wide alluvial basin of grassland crossed by rivers and ditches with pollarded willows; an unspoiled wetland rich in plants, birds and insects. The peat contains prehistoric trackways and settlements of international importance. Mainly dairy farming with some beef and sheep. *Threats from farming*: drainage, ploughing for arable farming, improvement of grassland. *Objectives of management*: maintain and improve wetland areas for wildlife by supporting livestock farming; safeguard archaeological remains.

South Downs

Characteristics: open chalk downland with rich grassland flora, insects and other invertebrates. Many surviving field patterns and archaeological remains from the Neolithic onwards. *Threats from farming*: ploughing or intensified management of grassland; encroachment of scrub; spray damage; and decay of buildings, walls and hedges. *Objectives of management*: maintain the quality of the turf by suitable grazing and scrub clearance. Protect wet valley grasslands from further damage. Conserve traditional landscape and archaeological features. Encourage the reconversion of arable to chalk grassland.

West Penwith

Characteristics: coastal strip of cliffs, heathland, farmland of small, walled or hedged fields with large granite boulders, bordered inland by moorland. Both coastal and inland heaths of

Deepdale and Dentdale in the Pennines, where improvements and intensification in agriculture threatened to destroy much of the beauty of the landscape and the wealth of wildlife, are now part of the Pennine Dales Environmentally Sensitive Area.

great interest for wildlife. An area which is exceptionally rich in archaeological remains. Farms small and engaged in specialist dairying. *Threats from farming*: reclamation of scrub and moor; neglect or removal of walls, hedges, narrow lanes and old buildings. *Objectives of management*: support small-scale dairying in order to preserve all these characteristic features.

Cambrian Mountains

Characteristics: extensive open hills of grassland and heath with enclosed farms and oakwoods in the valleys; hay meadows rich in wildflowers. Many upland birds especially the red kite. Extensive archaeological remains in farmland. Upland stock rearing for beef and sheep except for one-quarter which is afforested. *Threats from farming*: intensification of farming or afforestation; overburning of moorland. *Objectives of management*; safeguard archaeology; encourage the continuation of low-intensity stock rearing; enhance the quality of broadleaved woodlands.

Loch Lomond

Characteristics: the loch is the largest area of inland water in Britain - waterfalls, water-meadows, wooded promontories, bracken and heather, deciduous and conifer woodland - all contribute to the area's exceptional landscape value. Other features include the uplands which provide a good variety of habitats, notably scrub communities, muirs, heather, grasslands and extensive blanket bogs. There are also several features of archaeological interest including a scatter of sites and monuments around the loch. *Threats from farming*: increased grazing intensities would disturb the environmental quality of the open rough grazing. Afforestation may have landscape impact and threaten wildlife habitat. Native woodlands require protection from grazing. Water quality may deteriorate because of farm effluents. *Objects of management*: enhance the quality of the native woodlands, protect water quality, retain existing areas of heather, maintain the environmental quality of the rough grazings and ensure that new farm buildings are appropriately designed and sited.

Breadalbane

Characteristics: it is an area of hills interspersed with lochs, straths and glens. Traditional farm steadings and field boundaries contribute to its scenic value. Semi-natural woodland of broadleaves and Scots Pine are of especial scenic and wildlife importance. The arctic-alpine vegetation of the hills above Glen Lyon and Loch Tay are of special renown and the hills provide ranges for birds including the Golden Eagle and Merlin. There is considerable archaeological interest including stone circles, burial mounds and crannogs. *Threats from farming:* increased grazing levels may damage rough grazings and herbicide use reduce floristic quality. Similarly, lime and fertilisers could seriously disturb floristic diversity. Grazing in woods inhibits regeneration. *Objects of management*: enhance semi-natural woodlands, prevent reduction of floristic diversity, protect ranges of rare moorland birds, prevent pollution of water bodies and maintain landscape features such as field boundaries.

ADDRESSES

England and Wales

Countryside Commission for England and Wales,
John Dower House,
Crescent Place,
Cheltenham,
Glos. GL50 3RA

Regional offices:

> Office for Wales:
> Ladywell House,
> Newtown, Powys SY16 1RD

> Northern:
> Warwick House,
> Grantham Road,
> Newcastle upon Tyne NE2 1QF

> North West:
> 184 Deansgate,
> Manchester M3 3WB

> Yorkshire and Humberside:
> 8a Otley Road,
> Headingley,
> Leeds LS6 2AD

> Midlands:
> Cumberland House,
> Broad Street,
> Birmingham B15 1TD

> Eastern:
> Terrington House,
> 13-15 Hills Road,
> Cambridge CB2 1NL

> South West:
> Bridge House,
> Sion Place,
> Clifton Down,
> Bristol BS8 4AS

> South East:
> 30/32 Southampton Street,
> London WC2E 7RA

Nature Conservancy Council
Great Britain Headquarters,
Northminster House,
Peterborough PE1 1UA

Nature Conservancy Council
Headquarters for Wales,
Plas Penrhos,
Fford Penrhos,
Bangor,
Gwynedd LL57 2LQ

Forestry Commission,
231 Corstorphine Road,
Edinburgh EH12 7AT

Department of the Environment,
2 Marsham Street,
London SW1P 3EB

Welsh Office,
Cathays Park,
Cardiff CF1 3NQ

Ministry of Agriculture, Fisheries and Food,
Great Westminster House,
Horseferry Road,
London SW1P 2AE

Welsh Office Agriculture Department,
Plas Crug,
Aberystwyth,
Dyfed SY23 1NG

Association of County Councils,
Eaton House,
66a Eaton Square,
London SW1 9BH

National Trust,
36 Queen Anne's Gate,
London SW1H 9AS

English Heritage,
Fortress House,
23 Savile Row,
London W1X 3HE

Cadw,
Brunel House,
2 Fitzalan Road,
Cardiff CF2 1UY

Council for the Protection of Rural England,
4 Hobart Place,
London SW1W 0NY

Council for the Protection of Rural Wales,
31 High Street,
Welshpool,
Powys SY21 7JP

Scotland

Countryside Commission for Scotland,
Battleby,
Redgorton,
Perth PH1 3SW

Nature Conservancy Council,
Headquarters for Scotland,
12 Hope Terrace,
Edinburgh EH9 2AS

National Trust for Scotland,
5 Charlotte Square,
Edinburgh EH2 4DU

Association for the Protection of Rural Scotland,
14a Napier Road,
Edinburgh EH10 5AY

Scottish Wildlife Trust,
25 Johnston Terrace,
Edinburgh EH1 2NH

Department of Agriculture and Fisheries for Scotland,
Chesser House,
500 Gorgie Road,
Edinburgh EH11 3AW

Scottish Development Department,
Rural Environment and Nature Conservation Division,
New St Andrews House,
Edinburgh EH1 3SZ

Northern Ireland

Conservation Service,
Department of the Environment for Northern Ireland,
Calvert House,
23 Castle Place,
Belfast BT1 1FY

The National Trust,
Rowallane House,
Saintfield,
Ballynahinch,
Co. Down BT24 4LH

Others

Council for National Parks,
45 Shelton Street,
London WC2H 9HJ

Royal Society for Nature Conservation,
The Green,
Nettleham,
Lincoln LN2 2NR

Royal Society for the Protection of Birds,
The Lodge,
Sandy,
Beds SG19 2DL

Woodland Trust,
Autumn Park,
Dysart Road,
Grantham,
Lincs NG31 6LL

BIBLIOGRAPHY

Brecon Beacons National Park, *National Park Plan*, 1977.
Brecon Beacons National Park, *Draft National Park Plan, First Review*, 1986.
Carstairs, Ian, *North York Moors National Park*, Webb & Bower/Michael Joseph, 1987.
Countryside Commission, *New Agricultural Landscapes: issues, objectives and action*, CCP 102, 1977.
Countryside Commission, *A Review of Areas of Outstanding Natural Beauty*, CCP 140, 1980.
Countryside Commission, *Areas of Outstanding Natural Beauty; a policy statement*, CCP 157, 1983.
Countryside Commission, *Bibliography No.7: National Parks*, CCP 200, 1985.
Countryside Commission, *Public Enquiry on the proposed North Pennines Area of Outstanding Natural Beauty: Proof of evidence of the Countryside Commission*, 1985
Countryside Commission, *Heritage landscapes management plans*, CCP 205, 1986.
Countryside Commission, *Capital tax relief for outstanding scenic land*, CCP 204, 1986.
Countryside Commission, *A Better Future for the Uplands*, CCP 162, 1984.
Countryside Commission, *Annual Report 1984-85*, 1985.
Countryside Commission, *Annual Report 1985-86*, 1986.
Countryside Commission for Scotland, *Scotland's Scenic Heritage*, 1978.
Countryside Commission for Scotland, *A Park System for Scotland*, 1974.
Court, Glyn, *Exmoor National Park*, Webb & Bower/Michael Joseph 1987.
Dartmoor Commons Act 1985, HMSO, 1985.
Dartmoor National Park Authority, *Dartmoor National Park Plan*, 1977.
Dartmoor National Park Authority, *Dartmoor National Park Plan, First Review 1983*, 1983.
Dartmoor National Park Authority, *The Work of the Authority 1985-86*, 1986.
Department of the Environment, *Report of the National Parks Policies Review Committee (the Sandford Report)*, HMSO, 1974.
Department of the Environment, *A study of Exmoor*: report by Lord Porchester KBE to the Secretary of State for the Environment and the Minister of Agriculture, Fisheries and Food, November 1977, HMSO, 1977.
Exmoor National Park Committee, *Exmoor National Park Plan*, 1977.
Gill, Crispin (ed), *The Duchy of Cornwall*, David & Charles, 1987.
Green, Bryn, *Countryside Conservation*, Allen & Unwin, 1981.
Hampshire County Council, *Hampshire's Countryside Heritage: Ancient Woodland*, 1983.
Hopkins, Tony, *Northumberland National Park*, Webb & Bower/Michael Joseph, 1987.
Institute of Terrestrial Ecology, *Landscape Changes in Britain*, 1986.
Lacey, William S. (ed), *Britain's National Parks*, Windward, 1984.
Lake District National Park Authority, *National Park facts and figures*, 1986.
Lake District National Park Authority, *The Lake District National Park Plan, Reviewed 1986*, 1986.
Land Use Consultants, *The New Forest Landscape*, Countryside Commission, CCP 220, 1986.
Land Use Consultants, *A Planning Classification of Scottish Landscape*, Countryside Commission for Scotland, 1971.
Linton, D.L., "The assessment of scenery as a national resource", *Scottish Geographical Magazine*, 1968.
MacEwen, Ann and Malcolm, *National Parks: conservation or cosmetics?*, Allen & Unwin, 1982.
MacEwen, Ann and Malcolm, *Greenprints for the countryside?*, Allen & Unwin, 1987.
Ministry of Town & Country Planning, *National Parks in England and Wales (the Dower Report)*, Command Paper Cmd 6628, HMSO, 1945.
Ministry of Town & Country Planning, *Report of the National Parks Committee* (the Hobhouse Report), Command Paper Cmd 7121, HMSO, 1947.
Murdoch, John (ed), *The Lake District: A sort of national property*, Countryside Commission and Victoria & Albert Museum, CCP 194, 1986.
Murray, W.H., *Highland landscape; a survey*, National Trust for Scotland, 1962.
Northumberland National Park & Countryside Committee, *Northumberland National Park Plan*, 1977.
North York Moors National Park Committee, *North York Moors National Park Plan*, 1977.
North York Moors National Park Committee, *North York Moors National Park Plan, First Review*, 1984.

North York Moors National Park Committee, *Annual Report April 1985-March 1986*, 1986.

Peak Park Joint Planning Board, *Peak District National Park, National Park Plan*, 1978.

Park Park Joint Planning Board, *Annual Report No. 34, April 1985-March 1986*, 1986.

Pembrokeshire Coast National Park, *Functional Strategies 1987-1992*, 1986.

Pembrokeshire Coast National Park Authority, *Pembrokeshire Coast National Park Handbook*, 1983.

Pembrokeshire Coast National Park Committee, *Pembrokeshire Coast National Park Plan 1977-1982*, 1977.

Scottish Information Office, *Factsheet 5: Planning for Development*, 1984.

Scottish Information Office, *Local Government in Scotland*, 1984.

Scottish National Parks Survey Committee (Ramsay), *National Parks: a Scottish Survey*, Command paper Cmd 6631, HMSO, 1945.

Scottish National Parks Committee and the Scottish Wildlife Conservation Committee, *National Parks and the Conservation of Nature in Scotland*, Command paper Cmd 7235, HMSO, 1947.

Smith, Roland, *The Peak National Park*, Webb & Bower/Michael Joseph, 1987.

Snowdonia National Park Committee, *Snowdonia National Park Plan Draft*, 1977.

Styles, Showell, *Snowdonia National Park*, Webb & Bower/Michael Joseph, 1987.

Sumner, Heywood, (2nd edition), *A Guide to the New Forest*, 1925.

Thomas, Roger, *Brecon Beacons National Park*, Webb & Bower/Michael Joseph, 1987.

Tubbs, Colin R., *The New Forest, An Ecological History*, David & Charles, 1968.

Victoria & Albert Museum, *The Discovery of the Lake District*, 1984.

Waltham, Tony, *Yorkshire Dales National Park*, Webb & Bower/Michael Joseph, 1987.

Weir, John (ed.), *Dartmoor National Park*, Webb & Bower/Michael Joseph, 1987.

Williams, Herbert, *Pembrokeshire Coast National Park*, Webb & Bower/Michael Joseph, 1987.

Woodell, S.R.J. (ed.), "The English Landscape: past, present and future", *Wolfson College Lectures, 1983*. Oxford, 1983.

Wyatt, John, *The Lake District National Park*, Webb & Bower/Michael Joseph, 1987.

Yorkshire Dales National Park Committee, *Initial National Park Plan*, 1977.